UNSTOPPABLE

UNSTOPPABLE

David L. Black, PhD

This is book is dedicated to our grandchildren,
Ella, Maddie, Easton, Joey, Bear, and Dylan.
Love your Mimi as you know her,
and not as how others may try to define her.

TABLE OF CONTENTS

FOREWORD

On Tuesday, January 10, 2017, at the convening of the 110th Tennessee General Assembly, I passed the gavel to Randy McNally, my successor as Speaker of the Senate. It was a bittersweet moment for me, as I both looked forward to more time with my family and looked back fondly on the years I've served the people of our great state.

As a state senator, I enjoyed representing the people of my district and interceding on behalf of their needs. As lieutenant governor, it was my profound privilege to make a difference for citizens all across Tennessee. During the course of my twenty-four years in state government, first with the House of Representatives and then twenty years in the Senate, I had a center seat to political history on numerous occasions. I was the first Republican elected to serve as Speaker of the Senate in 140 years. I was the first Senate Speaker from my region, Sullivan County, in a century. And after a decade of wielding the gavel, I was the longest-serving Republican lieutenant governor in state history.

As notable as these historic milestones are, my proudest moments have been helping our party obtain supermajorities in both the House and Senate. Given that the Tennessee GOP had been the minority since the Civil War, few people believed we'd eventually turn this blue state red. Now that the Republican Party dominates the statehouse and the governor's mansion, we have good reason to ensure it stays that way. During my career as a legislator, I must have said a thousand times, "It matters who governs." We posted this adage on the wall of the Republican Caucus headquarters, and I displayed it on my desk. The Tennessee GOP trifecta has proven, and continues to prove, that it does matter who governs. We're making a difference.

Through various reforms and initiatives, the Tennessee legislature has brought prosperity, growth, and essential improvements to this great state. From a fiscal perspective, we have a budget surplus, our highway program is debt-free, and the pension fund is fully funded. I may be a little biased about this, but I believe we're the best-run state in the nation. I really do. In fact, the Mercatus Center at George Mason University ranked Tennessee in the top ten of the most financially healthy states in the nation.[1]

With the intent of drastically overhauling our educational system, the state legislature has also done some things that have been controversial. Tennessee crafted a comprehensive

---

1   "Ranking the States by Fiscal Condition 2017 Edition," Mercatus Center at George Mason University, posted July 11, 2017, https://www.mercatus.org/statefiscalrankings.

program of reforms that won our state a $500 million Race to the Top grant from the US Department of Education in 2010. Among our reforms were changes to the collective bargaining process for teachers, changes to how tenure is granted, and changes to how teachers' effectiveness in the classrooms is evaluated. We hoped these educational reforms would help us improve student achievement, and thanks to these initiatives, we are the fastest improving state in the nation.[2]

It really does matter who governs. Despite our successes to date, however, we can do more.

We achieved our sound fiscal position by passing conservative budgets and not spending more money than we have coming in. The improvements in Tennessee's education system didn't just happen under one governor but through the concerted efforts of one committed governor after another. Maintaining this upward trajectory will be the central challenge facing our next governor.

Therefore, it's important that we choose a leader who can stay the course and correct the course as needed. We need someone we can count on to strengthen our position as a pro-business state and improve our education system so that our residents can find their place in a thriving economy.

And I believe Diane Black is just the right person for the job.

I have known Diane since she was first sworn into the Tennessee House of Representatives in January of 1999.

2 "First to the Top," Tennessee Department of Education, accessed October 9, 2017, https://www.tn.gov/education/topic/first-to-the-top.

We seemed to hit it off from the very beginning—my first impression was that she was down to earth, a strong Christian, and committed to her family. Her eyes light up when she talks about her grandkids—we're a lot alike in that respect. But her sweet demeanor belies the sheer force of her personality when it comes to standing up for what's right.

Diane is indeed *unstoppable* when it comes to serving the people she has been elected to represent. She doesn't let much get in the way of her goals, and she isn't easily spooked when the odds are against her. As a state representative in 2003, she was audacious enough to run against the otherwise unopposed incumbent Speaker of the House, Democrat Jimmy Naifeh, just to make a point to her own party. She knew she would lose that vote, but her effort was a symbolic rebuke of electing a Speaker simply by acclamation.

When then-governor Don Sundquist tried to strong-arm legislators into implementing a state income tax, Diane was not intimidated in the least. She knew, like the majority of the legislature at the time, that the crux of Republican fiscal policy centers on a balanced budget and living within our means. Over the long haul, we've been proven correct. The state of Tennessee is booming, and it would have been a major mistake to adopt a state income tax at that time.

I've always considered Diane Black to be one of the most effective legislators in our state government. In 2004, I talked her into running for the 18th Senate District seat, even though she was happy serving in the House and polls revealed she would have tough competition against the incumbent. But Diane won that election and furthered the Tennessee GOP's mission to finally gain the majority in the Senate. Her leadership abilities were so evident that, in 2006, we elected her the Tennessee Senate Republican Caucus chairman—the first woman to ever hold that position.

I'll admit, when she decided she wanted to run for Congress in 2010, I tried to talk her out of it because she was doing such a great job in the state legislature. But she continues to make history on the federal level—she became the first woman and the first Tennessean to chair the House Budget Committee, which scored a major victory in passing the 2018 budget resolution.

I foresee that there will be certain individuals on the gubernatorial campaign trail who will try to paint Diane as an establishment Republican from Washington, DC. That's what I might do if I were her opponent, given how wary people are of experienced politicians. But Diane is a true public servant. The usual political campaign tricks can't stack up against her proven track record of conservative achievements at both the state and federal levels.

More than anyone else in the gubernatorial race, Diane truly embodies the conservative principles and philosophies of the people of the state of Tennessee. She has the experience and relationships to get things done that no one else on the campaign trail has.

As a person, they just don't come any better—her Christian values shine through in everything she does.

Anyone who knows Diane also knows that, beyond her fiscal conservatism, she is passionate about the pro-life movement. She brought both her Christian faith and her knowledge as a medical professional to her effort to amend the Tennessee constitution that put decisions about abortion back into the hands of the lawmakers rather than in the courts.

Diane has been a force for good in our state and our nation. In *Unstoppable*, Diane's husband, Dave Black, has captured the heart and spirit of this dynamic woman in a way only he could. I am confident that, once you've read this book, you will see the genuine character behind the public figure, and you will see the truth behind the political falsehoods.

It has been my distinct privilege to be a part of Tennessee history, and I am proud to support Diane Black in her own historic bid for governor. My greatest hope for her time as governor is that she will continue to keep our great state on the trajectory we're on right now—I am confident that she is the choice candidate to do that and even improve upon the gains we've made.

As Diane is known to say, she'll "git 'er done," with the grace and dignity for which she is known.

—Ron Ramsey, Former Lieutenant Governor and Speaker of the Senate
Blountville, Tennessee

October 30, 2017

INTRODUCTION

The first time I ever laid eyes on Diane Lynn Warren, I knew there was something special about her. It was a Saturday night in October of 1967, and both of us were on dates with other people. But in the brief moment we met, I could see in Diane an inner vitality and liveliness that I would never forget. She was not just pretty—she had a visible energy about her.

At the time, I was nineteen years old and a freshly minted Marine. I had been at various training camps over the course of the prior year and had recently arrived at the Marine Corps Air Station at Cherry Point, North Carolina. The day I checked into Cherry Point, I was in the barracks unloading gear from my seabag when across the aisle a guy named Marvin walked over and introduced himself.

"I'm going on liberty soon," he said, "and if you want to come with me, I'll fix you up on a date."

Agreeing to travel from Cherry Point, North Carolina, to Baltimore, Maryland, on a four-day pass for a blind date was way out of character for me. But the trip and the blind date were perhaps a natural response to what felt like a very unnatural time in my life. My high school sweetheart had recently broken my heart after three years of dating. She was the first girl I had ever loved, and the breakup bruised and damaged a lot of who I thought I was. And being a Marine in 1967 meant that a trip to Vietnam was not far off in my future. This was the time to live life and take a chance.

Marvin had arranged for me to take a sophomore named Anna to her Homecoming dance at Andover High School in Linthicum, Maryland, a small town just outside of Baltimore. When Marvin and I took the bus to Baltimore, I didn't realize we were going well out of bounds—the liberty pass only allowed us to travel as far north as Washington, DC—but as long as we made it back on time, we were unlikely to get into any serious trouble.

Anna's parents put me up in their guest room and lent me their old Mercedes so I could drive us to the weekend festivities. We went to a football game earlier that Saturday and then headed to the Homecoming dance that night. The school year was well into the fall semester—the night air was crisp, and the tree leaves were hanging on to the colors of autumn.

We ended up being late to the Homecoming dance because Anna wanted to stop by a local gas station to say hello to a guy named Oats who was working there. I waited in the car while she went inside the gas station to talk to him for fifteen minutes. That certainly did not start the date on a promising note. And arriving late meant parking in the distant recesses of the high school parking lot. Anna wasn't happy about that, and she made a negative remark or two that didn't further enhance the moment.

The tension eased as we entered a packed and dimly lit gymnasium teeming with several hundred decked-out teenagers milling around, talking, and dancing to the sounds of Motown. Dressed in my Marine Corps winter greens, I believe I was the only young man in uniform, although I didn't have much other clothing anyway. I thought I looked pretty good though; I was certainly physically fit and figured on occasion I might get a second look from a pretty girl. I was, however, still rather shy.

As it turned out, I was the one who ended up doing a double take when I finally met Diane. I first saw her shortly after Anna and I had entered the gym. To the left of us was a table where two couples were already comfortably settled with appetizers and sodas. They all sat in a row with their backs to the wall.

"Dave, these are my friends," Anna said. "This is Steve and Diane, and this is Tracy and Tom."

These four young people would later become friends of mine, but in the moment the only person I saw and paid any real attention to was Diane. She was a pretty, sixteen-year-old sophomore, but it wasn't her beauty-queen looks that got to me. I could tell she was special and quite extraordinary.

It's hard to put into words the qualities that radiated from her that were so immediately attractive.

Diane and I only got a chance to speak briefly—not much more than a hello and a few words about my being a Marine from Michigan—before Anna and I moved on to talk to other people. Later in life, Diane would enjoy telling folks that she did not remember meeting me, even though I was sharply dressed in my Marine Corps winter greens. But I never forgot the moment I first encountered her. I met a lot of other young people that night, but she's the only one I could have later picked out of a crowd and named by name.

In the ensuing years that followed the 1967 Andover High School Homecoming, I married Anna—despite the rough start to our first date—and Diane married Steve. Tom and Tracy got married too, and we would all run into each other from time to time at events around town.

Despite the strong impression Diane made on me that October night in 1967, I could never have imagined at the time that we would later embark on a life together. Eleven years after that Homecoming dance, we were both single again; we reconnected, dated, and got married, and I adopted the three beautiful children she'd had with Steve.

Over the course of this book, I want to share with you this remarkable story and more about the special woman at the center of it all.

From public housing to public office

When Diane announced her candidacy for governor of Tennessee, Steve Stivers, chairman of the National Republican Congressional Committee, said, "Diane Black is a force of nature and is simply unstoppable. Her work in the House, and specifically on the Budget Committee, has been pivotal to what we've been able to accomplish. I'm proud to be able to call her my friend, and I will miss her tenacity. I wish her and her family the best of luck in her future endeavors."

Diane is indeed *unstoppable*. Throughout her life, she has demonstrated this truth about her character. When her mind and heart are set in a certain direction, not much holds her back—that's just who she is.

Diane's personal story is a classic example of the American Dream. She was born to working-class, Depression-era parents. She spent her earliest years living in public housing in a poor neighborhood south of Baltimore and later grew up in a small white house along with her three siblings. Despite her family's tough circumstances, Diane was unstoppable in pursuing her dream of attaining an education. Thanks to a caring and highly involved high school counselor, Mr. Whiting, she broke the mold to become the first person in her family to earn a college degree.

After her first husband succumbed to alcoholism and abandoned their marriage, Diane was unstoppable in stepping up to care for her three children on her own. She is no stranger to hard work—Diane and I both know firsthand what it's like to barely scrape by, to work day and night just to make ends meet. We both grew up poor, and we both started working at age twelve to help our families. Despite the hardships we endured, we believed that with hard work and determination—the old-fashioned, American way—we could overcome our circumstances.

That shared value was evident not just in our childhoods but was our standard way of life as young adults and then as a married couple. While continuing her nursing career, Diane ran multiple small businesses to help support our family when I was finishing graduate school. After we moved to Tennessee in 1986, Diane was again unstoppable as she pursued a four-year nursing degree, while still raising our three children and working full-time to support our family during the years I first started Aegis Sciences Corporation. Everything that we have achieved over the years has been the result of working together and supporting each other in our endeavors.

Diane's experiences as a nurse inspired her to enter state government in order to help stabilize and reform the flailing and unsustainable TennCare program. When she first ran for the Tennessee House of Representatives in 1998, Diane was unstoppable against an opponent who was a member of an old Sumner County family with strong, nationwide political connections that provided financial support and outspent her campaign two to one. Diane was also unstoppable when she first ran for the Tennessee Senate in 2004 against the most powerful female Democrat in the state. No one thought Diane could win, and though she again was greatly outspent, she took the seat and helped give the Republicans their first state senate majority in Tennessee history.

Diane has been most publicly unstoppable in her dedication to pro-life causes. Throughout her time in the General Assembly, she fought to advance a constitutional amendment that would allow our elected representatives to enact commonsense abortion laws to protect women and the unborn.

When she first ran for Congress in 2010, Diane was unstoppable in the face of a well-financed smear campaign of utter lies during the Republican primary. In Congress, she has remained unstoppable in her dedication to advancing the pro-life agenda, repealing and replacing Obamacare, and working to bring fiscal sanity back to Washington.

Diane does not go halfway—ever. When she goes into something, she does it 110 percent. Therefore, it hasn't surprised me in the least that in every office she occupies— whether in the state legislature or the US Congress—she is placed in positions of authority and leadership. Her rise among the ranks has been the result of her effectiveness, not because she engaged in games or political ploys. She combines her limitless energy with a devotion to "doing the right thing" for her family, church, community, state, and nation.

Diane entered politics not out of any hunger for power or a vision for status and prestige. She was, above all else, driven to make a difference. She is the most selfless person I have ever known. She is grounded by her faith and her humility. Those who know her well know this is true about her. People have come to her with significant issues, and she has managed to turn them into meaningful policy and effective legislation, many times in the face of significant opposition. She is strong and independent—a quality I have always loved about her—and she can pick up a cause and truly make something come of it. Although she has served in public office for nearly twenty years, she has successfully resisted becoming a "politician." She still believes she is there to serve, not to be served.

A refute of false narratives

We live in a time when character assassination is par for the course in any political campaign, no matter how localized that campaign might be. Rather than merely debate the issues, some people are determined to destroy their opponent's reputation. Over the nearly two decades that my wife has been in public service, we have encountered these false narratives repeatedly. We've read about them in political mailers. We've seen the attack ads on TV and through social media. We've had awful things spoken directly to us. This seems to be the way of modern politics, though we truly wish it weren't so.

It is painful to see your loved one slandered, especially when you know the truth about their character and integrity. I have spoken out on my wife's behalf in the past, and I feel compelled to do so again as she runs the race to be Tennessee's next governor.

Diane didn't ask me to write this book—in fact, she didn't even know about it until it was completed and ready to be published. But as her husband, I believe I'm in the best position to speak about Diane's true character. I've known her for fifty years, and I've been married to her for more than thirty-seven of those years. I'm a forensic scientist by training and nature, and I believe that despite my deep and enduring love for her, I can be objective and remain focused on the facts. If I do get a bit sentimental on occasion, well, I trust you'll indulge me a little. I'm definitely the romantic one in the relationship.

When my wife felt the conviction to enter her first political contest, we both prayed over the decision. We are people of deep faith, so we trusted God for guidance. I often joke that her prayer was answered; mine was not. I sensed that this would be a challenging journey for her and for our family. But from the beginning, I have supported her every step of the way, and I've been exceedingly proud of her achievements in the years since.

Over the past thirty years, Diane Black has devoted countless hours of her time, immeasurable amounts of energy, and the best of her heart and mind to her local community, the state of Tennessee, and the greater good of the nation. I'm honored to call her my wife, and I hope that as you read this biography you will get to know more fully this strong, independent woman who indeed has been an unstoppable force for good.

[Author's Note: Names of some of the people portrayed in this book have been changed to protect their privacy.]

CHAPTER 1

MEAGER BEGINNINGS

Diane and I have lived in Tennessee now for more than thirty years. We've made lifelong friends along the way, but we've gained our share of critics as well. Those who don't know us intimately might see our current success without realizing the long, hard road we took to get to where we are.

Diane and I each grew up poor and had to start working at a young age to help our families get by. For many years Diane was reluctant to share the story of how she grew up for fear of how she might be judged, but when she started opening up, she discovered other people had lived similar stories. This openness has forged personal connections that have made her grateful for her own childhood experiences, which she now shares freely.

Diane Lynn Warren was born on January 16, 1951, to Joseph and Audrey Warren in Westport, a neighborhood in south Baltimore, Maryland. Joe and Audrey are typical folks of the Greatest Generation who grew up during the Great

Depression. Joe had only a sixth grade education, and Audrey only made it through ninth grade.

Diane's dad is a veteran of the Second World War. He built airstrips in the Marshall Islands as part of the Seabees, the nickname for the United States Naval Construction Battalion, or "CBs," and was shipped to the Pacific theater when he was only eighteen. Though he wasn't in frontline combat, he participated in the surrender of a Japanese unit on one of the islands. He still has a Japanese rifle and the flag brought down from the flagpole that his commanding officer gave him as keepsakes.

Joe and Audrey fell in love while they were both working on the assembly line of a paper-box factory in a poorer section of Baltimore. Diane was the third of four children, and when she arrived into the world, her family was living in public housing. While public housing back then wasn't quite as rough as it later became, the house they lived in was a row home on Wilgrey Court in a rather rundown part of Baltimore. Joe was an electrician, a trade he first learned in the Navy, but he just couldn't make much money at the time—it wasn't all that easy right after World War II to find a job. He was never a man to sit around, however, and he eventually managed to obtain decent jobs to support his family with companies like McCormick Spice and Kaiser Aluminum.

Life in Ferndale

When Diane was about five years old, Joe moved the family from the brownstone in Westport to a small white house in Ferndale that was built after World War II. Though Diane was little when they lived in public housing, she has memories of a swing set and playing with kids in a nearby alley. The new house, though an improvement for everyone, lacked these particular amenities, which young Diane found discouraging.

That part of Anne Arundel County was very rural back then, and the Warrens' new home was one of the first in an area that had once been farmland. Ferndale was a small, working-class community. Diane has said she lived on the other side of the tracks—which she did, quite literally. There were train tracks several blocks from her house on which large locomotives rumbled loudly on their way through town.

The house she grew up in, along with her parents and three siblings, was exceedingly small—less than fifteen hundred square feet. I struggle to understand how Joe and Audrey managed to raise four children in that house, but they did. It only took about three strides to get from one side to the other. On the first floor were a living room, bathroom, two small bedrooms, and a kitchen that they later expanded. The second level was an attic that they eventually finished enough to add two more bedrooms, but if you had to use the bathroom you had to go back down the steep set of stairs to the first floor. The steep-pitched roof meant that if you walked too far from the center of the attic space, you hit your head on the ceiling.

To this day, Joe and Audrey still live in that little white house. During the early 1980s, when fuel costs were skyrocketing in the area, Joe removed all the asphalt shingles from the exterior, installed sheets of insulation, and reset the shingles on the house. With the shingles removed, the outside of the house was just two-by-fours, and it was evident the old blown-in insulation had settled to the bottom of the frame.

Joe is a doer, and he is very frugal. I'm sure Diane inherited a lot of his personality. Like her dad, she could squeeze a penny and make ole Abe Lincoln scream. To this day, she rarely buys clothes or other things unless they're on sale. The result of Joe's insulation installation project served to not only better insulate the home, but also left it virtually without any airflow or air turnover. My brother-in-law and I used to joke that we had to go outside just to breathe. He even once said, "You could fart in this house in November, and it wouldn't get out of the house until spring."

A little leader

Diane has two older brothers, Joe Jr. and Doug, and a younger sister named Pattie. When she was little, Diane shared a bed with her brothers—usually sleeping right in the middle— while her baby sister slept in a crib nearby. Diane certainly suffered as a younger sister to two big brothers.

"They teased the living hell out of me," she said with a laugh.

As the Warren kids grew up, they were quite the pack of troublemakers. One of the stories Diane loves to tell is about the time she and her brothers put up a tire swing in the woods in the back of the house. She wanted to try it out first, so her brothers twisted the swing around and around and around until the rope was almost one large knot. When they released it with her inside the tire, she spun so fast she got sick, and the boys had to carry her into the house.

In another instance, Joe and Doug pretended they were having a home fire drill, and everyone had to escape from the second floor via the window. Diane went first this time too—helped by a shove from her brothers. The fire drill ended with a visit to the ER where Diane had to get stitches in her tongue. Amazingly she was not seriously hurt.

The boys were pretty wild, but it was back in a time when boys were expected to be that way. Joe and Doug used to throw the fish they caught into the aboveground swimming pool in the backyard. When I first met Diane's folks and saw the pool in the backyard, it was not a pretty sight! They even had a pet squirrel in the basement at one point that would crawl into their old billiard table and go into, and pop up from, the pockets.

"Why in the world do you play with them?" Audrey would ask Diane about her brothers. But her daughter was having too much fun to mind, and she was tough enough to tolerate their abuse.

If the boys were expected to be wild, the girls were expected to be submissive, though I don't think Diane ever got that memo. From a young age, she was always a person in charge—I have warned people that she's never been a member of any organization that she didn't end up leading. Even as a child, she was the one trying to organize and direct her siblings, cousins, and friends on where to be and what to do.

When I asked Diane's mom about her daughter's personality as a child, Audrey just laughed and said, "She was always independent, always a leader. No one could tell her what to do. It was always her way that things had to be done. Even when very young, she wanted to take charge." Diane's mother has old family 35 mm film that shows Diane clearly directing family members on what to do no matter what the occasion might have been.

Given Joe's work schedule, there were many times he wasn't present with the children. When he worked the night shift, he slept during the day, so it had to be quiet around the house. Though Audrey didn't work and was present in the home, Diane learned from a young age to fend for herself. When she was twelve, she started working for the first time. There was a woman who lived in the largest house in their neighborhood who was fond of her. The lady and her husband mentored her, and she earned money cleaning their home. When Diane was fifteen, the lady hired her to work at the dry cleaner that she and her husband owned in Ferndale.

Despite the limited resources, Diane has always reminisced that her childhood was full of love. Joe is a kind, gentle man, and a man of faith—he and Audrey brought up the children faithfully attending the Lutheran church, which was within walking distance from their home. Her father had five siblings, and her mother had nine, and the extended families often came together for backyard feasts of deep-fried crab and steamed crab, or long days water-skiing on an old ironing board on the Chesapeake Bay. One of her great uncles on her father's side, Bill Lee, used to make large vats of spaghetti and throw just about anything in the pot along with the noodles, even things like steamed blue crab. I'm not sure I'd want blue crab in my pasta, but he was a child of the Great Depression—if it was edible, you ate it. Uncle Bill nicknamed Diane "Dapper Dan" after the racehorse who competed on the local Pimlico Race Course, because he said Dapper Dan was quick and beautiful.

Diane spent a lot of time with her many cousins, and she tells stories about how close she was to her aunts and uncles. Her mother's mother was an old-time Baptist. On Sundays, her grandmother would have the family over for dinner, and she played piano and sang hymns, which Diane remembers fondly. She still comes to tears when she hears those old hymns played in church, like "Amazing Grace" or "The Old Rugged Cross." She can hear her grandmother in her memories, and it just overwhelms her.

The doctor's kit

Diane knew from a young age that she wanted to be a nurse when she grew up. When she was about four years old, she asked her family for a doctor's kit. It wasn't typical back then for a woman to be a doctor, but there were no "nurse's kits" then. She very well could have been a doctor—she's the best medical professional I know. After years of emergency room experience, she can diagnose better than most doctors.

As a little girl with her new doctor's kit, she acted as the physician on her siblings and other willing playmates. But girls in the 1950s were expected to marry and have babies, not enter demanding professions. Diane has said that people back then just didn't know how to dream.

Ferndale didn't have a kindergarten at the time, so Diane started school in the first grade. She walked to school with her older brothers and eventually with friends even at such a young age. The school was across Baltimore-Washington Boulevard, which today is a busy road, and across the train tracks—about a mile from her house, which is a pretty good walk for a first grader. It's not something that would be done today.

Later in high school, Diane crossed the tracks again from the poorer section of town where her family lived to attend Andover High School in Linthicum Heights. Growing up, Diane didn't have a sense of being poor because not many people around her had much either. Living below the tracks didn't make her feel poor so much as it made her feel different.

She didn't realize she was part of a lower income community until she went to high school.

In Linthicum Heights, there was a clear divide between Diane and her middle-class classmates. Anna—my date to the Homecoming dance—drove a Mercedes, a newer model than the one I later borrowed from her dad, while Diane rode the bus to school. Anna was like a lot of kids at that school who had credit cards and spending money and could go out and have fun, while Diane sewed and cleaned houses for cash.

Despite the economic differences, Diane had a lot of friends and was very active at Andover. She was a basketball player and a gymnast, and during her junior year she was even a princess on the Teen Court. According to Audrey, Diane's high school offered two tracks—academic or business—perhaps similar to today's system in terms of college prep or vocational training. Diane only wanted to follow the academic program. She had taken an aptitude test that confirmed her natural abilities—the results said she should go into nursing or engineering. She was quite mechanically inclined, but she loved taking care of people, and nursing had been her childhood dream.

Diane's parents, however, couldn't support her hopes of going to nursing school.

"How can you go to college?" Audrey said. "We don't have the money for that."

But Diane has always been determined in everything she does—she knew she wanted to go to college, so she would have to find her own way. Thankfully someone else saw something special in her and helped usher her dream into reality.

During her freshman year, Diane met Richard Whiting, one of Andover High School's guidance counselors. He was grandfatherly with his gray hair and sweet demeanor, and he was the only school staff member who wore a suit and tie every day. Mr. Whiting noticed Diane's potential and took her under his wing, encouraging her to keep up her good grades and to keep her sights set on college.

Mr. Whiting was a good man and loved kids—he ran the Linthicum Teen Center and spent his Saturday nights supervising teens who enjoyed a safe place to spend time. Diane began volunteering at the center, helping set up the facility, changing the music records on the turntable, and cleaning up at the end. Mr. Whiting often took his volunteers out for burgers after the center closed for the evening, which helped Diane get to know him more personally.

"These were some of the best times we had, this small group of kids who were really close to Mr. and Mrs. Whiting," said Diane. "Can you imagine sacrificing every Saturday night to hang out with a bunch of teenagers? He was really special."

When she was a sophomore, he started asking her about her plans for college.

"I don't see how that's possible," she responded. "My parents don't have any money to pay for me to go to college."

Given their own lack of education, Diane's parents would have been thrilled if their children simply finished high school—seeing beyond that was difficult for them. But Mr. Whiting knew Diane wanted to be a nurse.

"You're going to nursing school," he said. "We're going to find a way."

Mr. Whiting meant what he said, and he began nominating her for scholarships to civic groups in the area.

"Mr. Whiting saw something in me I didn't see in myself," Diane said. "He was like a father figure to me—he really cared. And not just me, he cared about a lot of young people in our school. That's just who he was."

When she was a senior, she got called to the guidance counselor's office. When she arrived, Mr. Whiting announced she had been named "Girl of the Year" by the local Optimist Club.

"And there's more," he said. "Here's a check for one thousand dollars to go with it!"

Diane screamed and started jumping up and down right there in his office.

After she graduated high school, that scholarship covered the costs of her first year of nursing school. She continued to work her way through college doing the same odd jobs she'd done as a teenager—sewing clothes and cleaning homes— and paid the rest of her way through her second year. Like her father, Diane is a doer and not one to sit around.

Mr. Whiting was present at Diane's graduation ceremony when she received her associate's degree in nursing from Anne Arundel Community College in Arnold, Maryland, in

1971. He believed in her, and his encouragement and support was essential to her advancement out of Ferndale. He opened doors for her that may never have otherwise opened, and that has made all the difference in Diane's life.

"I don't think I would be where I am today if it weren't for Mr. Whiting," Diane said.

To demonstrate the depth of her appreciation, Diane made Mr. Whiting godfather to her daughter Jill when she was born in 1975. Mr. Whiting died a few years later.

Growing up dirt poor

Though this book is about Diane, I want to share how much my upbringing paralleled hers, albeit a bit worse. Both of us came from nothing, and in contrast to the hardships, our lives have turned out to be quite the American Dream.

I grew up mostly in Wayne, Michigan. While Diane lived in public housing, my stock line is that my family *aspired* to live in public housing. We weren't dirt poor—we couldn't even afford dirt. At one point we had so little money that we lived in a rented mobile home in a trailer park that was likely subsidized by the state of Michigan. By the time I was eighteen, my family had lived in nineteen different places. I thought it was normal to move out of a place in the middle of the night, which we did because my father would skip rent.

When we were moving back to Michigan from Elkhart, Indiana, the Indiana State Police pulled us over and took my father out of the car to speak with him. I was left alone in the car for some time, although I was only seven or eight years old, and only learned later in life that he was advised to not return to the state. I am sure there is much more to that story than I will ever know.

Like Diane's dad, my father, Donald Eugene Black, didn't have a high school education. He was also a World War II veteran in the Pacific, but unlike Joe, my dad saw combat up close and ugly. He was stationed on the USS Pringle, a Fletcher-class destroyer. His ship had been previously hit by suicide aircraft, an attack that killed ten men, but then during the Battle of Okinawa, they were hit by two or three kamikazes in a row. Six minutes later, the ship sank. My father saw sixty-nine of his buddies killed, and another seventy were wounded. He was one of 258 survivors who were circled by sharks before they were finally pulled out of the water. I learned only recently that while the sailors were in the water, they were strafed by American fighter aircraft. The men thought they were being mistaken for Japanese and were angry until they learned later that the pilots were strafing the sharks to protect them.

My father met my mother, Marion, in Treasure Island, California, while they were both in the Navy. She was part of the women's reserve, known as WAVES (Women Accepted for Volunteer Emergency Service). My older sister was born while my parents were still in the Navy. Her name, if you can believe it, is Diane Lynn Black—just like my wife. I was the second born and oldest boy, and then I had three younger brothers named Donny, Danny, and Dale.

Like most veterans of the era, my father wouldn't talk about what happened during the war. No one back then really discussed the psychological damage the veterans suffered. Instead of talking, my dad drank. He was a true, committed alcoholic. I don't know what demons he lived with; I wasn't in his skin and I couldn't walk in his shoes and I have tried hard not to judge him. But he was so intoxicated for most of my childhood that I couldn't bring friends home for fear of what state he'd be in. He was mean, abusive, neglectful. I still have scars on my back from the beatings. He was not a loving father—in fact, he was a role model for me in what not to be as a man and father.

By the time I might have started asking questions about what had happened to my father during the war, I had to find work to help support my mother and my siblings. He often disappeared for days and weeks at a time. It was the winter of 1960, and it was bitterly cold out. We had no food in the house, no heat, and something had to be done. I was twelve years old and six feet tall. I had grown so fast the prior summer that my legs ached and throbbed, especially at night, and I often lay in bed crying.

I managed to find a job washing cars at a local gas station alongside a college kid named Hap. Each wash cost fifty cents; Hap kept a quarter because he was older and the real muscle, the gas station took fifteen cents, and I earned ten cents. One Roosevelt dime for each car washed. And let me tell you— washing cars in Wayne, Michigan, in the wintertime ain't easy. We pulled cars into the bay to wash off the dirt and salt, then back outside to dry off, but we had to move fast before the water froze! If I worked really hard on a Saturday or Sunday, I could make $2 or $3 to take home to my mother. Although that does not sound like much, back then a dozen eggs or a loaf of bread was about nineteen cents. A gallon of gas was about fifteen cents. I don't remember the cost of coal, but probably not much. So those few dollars went a long way.

I worked at the gas station for several years, washing cars, pumping gas, and eventually making mechanical repairs such as replacing mufflers and doing tune-ups. In high school, I worked virtually full-time every evening after school— stocking produce in a grocery store, delivering frozen foods, landscaping and cutting grass. I worked a lot of different jobs that taught me a lot of good life lessons.

When Diane said she didn't perceive herself as poor when she was a child, at first I agreed. But then I remembered how my clothes always had holes in them (long before that was cool!), and even though I was the eldest boy, my clothes were almost always secondhand. My shoes were also almost always too small, which is why I have curled toes to this day (I'm surprised the Marines even took me given how deformed my feet are). I remember going through a Michigan winter without a winter coat or gloves, wearing layers of sweaters to try to stay warm. Before I started working at the gas station, I had joined the Boy Scouts. While the other kids got new uniforms, I was taken to the church basement and given an old, used uniform that smelled bad and fit poorly.

I do, in fact, remember the shame of being poor.

The children in our neighborhood taunted me for wearing ratty clothing and teased me because my father was a drunk. The kids called me racial slurs because my last name was Black. I detested the "n" word long before I even knew how racist it was or what it was supposed to mean, and it sensitized me at a young age to anyone who experienced bigotry.

Even my father made racist remarks that offended me when I was young. My father lived angry most of the time I knew him. Later in life, he found his Christian faith, but it was long after all of his children had been deeply scarred by the experience. All of my siblings used various forms of drugs, beginning with marijuana and then graduating to much harder substances, to cope with the pain of our upbringing. Two of them have died of overdoses—my sister, Diane, died first, at age forty-seven, from a mixture of pharmaceutical drugs. Because she and my wife had the exact same name, we couldn't put her death notice in our church bulletin for fear of confusion. My brother Danny died at forty-five of a heroin overdose.

As for me, I didn't want to end up like my father—a man who didn't provide for his family, abused his wife, and harmed his children. I wanted an education, and since my family had no money, I would have to find my own way as well.

I graduated from high school on a Thursday night, and on Friday morning, I joined the Marine Corps. I had always been patriotic, and my Michigan high school education was excellent at teaching civics and American history. I also watched way too many John Wayne movies, and deep down I wanted to be Sgt. John Stryker in *Sands of Iwo Jima*. But most importantly, the GI Bill would be my ticket to college.

After boot camp in San Diego and infantry training at Camp Pendleton, California, I was assigned to the Marine Air Wing and spent nine months at the Millington Air Station in Memphis, Tennessee, training in aviation electronics. After that, I ended up at the Marine Corps Air Station at Cherry Point, North Carolina, and soon made my way to Baltimore where I first crossed paths with Diane Lynn Warren that October night in 1967 at the Andover High School Homecoming dance.

In June of 1968, I was ordered to Vietnam where I spent thirteen months coming under small arms fire and rocket fire at Danang and Chu Lai. This was the height of the Vietnam War and was one of the experiences in life that shaped my character forever. I flew out of Danang to come home on July 4, 1969, and everything I owned in the world was in my seabag.

Many years of life and several more chapters of this story lie between that era and the present one. Reuniting with Diane eleven years later and then journeying together as a family has been the central joy of my life.

Though Diane and I have enjoyed substantial success since our meager beginnings, neither of us has forgotten where we came from. I like to think I'm still blue collar because I came from a blue-collar family and had my earliest job in the automobile industry. To this day I keep a 1960 Roosevelt dime on me constantly to remind me of how much work it represents and to keep me grounded. When we gave $1 million to the Volunteer State Community College to build the new humanities building, that was 10 million dimes to me. Ten million car washes to a twelve-year-old. And I keep my seabag in my office to remind me of coming home from war thankful for surviving and realizing that I don't need any more stuff than what fits into a seabag to get through life and be happy.

And I think it's hard for people to appreciate that Diane is still the same person she was when I met her—she's still the vibrant sixteen-year-old I met in Ferndale. You would think with all of her success that she might have ended up with a supersized ego, but she's still that humble, somewhat hesitant girl I met and later came to love.

CHAPTER 2

A LOVE STORY

The three couples who met the night of the Homecoming dance in 1967—Anna and me, Steve and Diane, Tom and Tracy—all married and started their young adult lives in different ways.

I returned from Vietnam in July of 1969, not long after Anna and Diane had graduated from Andover High School, and Anna and I were married that August. Diane and Steve, her high school sweetheart, were married on June 6, 1970, after her first year in nursing school, and they had the first of their three children, Steve Jr., the November after she graduated in 1971.

In the fall of 1970, I was discharged from active duty from the Marines, and Anna and I moved up to Ypsilanti, Michigan, where I spent a year at Eastern Michigan University. We only lasted a year there, however, because my family kept up a constant pace of drama that interrupted my life and studies, and Anna wanted to be closer to her parents. We moved back to Maryland, and I enrolled in Loyola College (now a university) in Baltimore. I loved studying and learning, and I finished in 1974 with a bachelor of science in biology and a minor in chemistry.

While I was studying at Loyola, we didn't see Steve, Diane, Tom, and Tracy all that often, though Anna and I ran into them at the Glen Burnie Carnival one summer night in 1971, and I went fishing from time to time with Steve and other fishing buddies.

Like Diane, I ended up being the only one in my family with a college education. After I completed my undergraduate degree, I enrolled in a doctorate program in forensic toxicology at the University of Maryland School of Medicine. My research focused on the toxicology and pathology of *Cannabis sativa* (marijuana). Despite the fact that my father was an alcoholic, my mother was addicted to Valium, and all my siblings were drug users who began with marijuana, my family was not the inspiration behind my choosing to study substance abuse. It was simply that marijuana was having a wide impact at the time, especially with veterans returning from the Vietnam War.

While I was in graduate school, I worked in a laboratory that conducted emergency toxicology tests for local hospitals, one of which was St. Agnes Hospital in Baltimore where Diane worked in the emergency room. Hospitals like hers sent patient blood, urine, and gastric samples in cases of suspected overdose, and after I'd done the toxicology testing, I reported my results to the doctor or nurse who had submitted the sample. Once they knew what drugs the person had in their system, they could devise a proper treatment plan as needed. In many calls to St. Agnes to deliver my reports, I ended up talking to Diane without even realizing it! We figured out over time that it was *the* Diane from Ferndale. Long before we kindled a personal relationship, we had a professional rapport, even though we didn't know it right away.

Sometime in 1975, Anna and I were helping Tom and Tracy move into a row home. Diane and Steve were there with their second child, Jill, who was just a newborn—I even remember holding her. Steve was drinking heavily that day and became intoxicated. I'd seen him drink a lot on past occasions, but this was the first time I'd seen him completely drunk. Both of Steve's parents were alcoholics, so he'd come out of a family not much more stable than mine. Diane pled with him to go home, but he wouldn't listen.

I don't know what the precipitating moment of Steve's decline was, but he only got worse from there. Steve was physically and verbally abusive. He was also abusive to the children and did things like teach them profane words to repeat to their mother.

For seven years, Diane struggled to keep her marriage together, but in 1977, when she became pregnant with her third child, Steve decided to leave. He didn't want another child—in fact, he urged her to end her pregnancy. Diane was devastated by his sudden departure, but her next thought was caring for her babies. She and Steve sold their house in Annapolis, and Diane bought a small house in front of her childhood home where her parents still lived in Ferndale. Now a single mother to three small children, she worked multiple shifts at the hospital to support her family.

My own marriage fell apart before Diane and Steve's did. Anna and I were unable to have children of our own and had agreed we would adopt instead. I had always loved children, and I wanted a family no matter how it came into being. Back when I was in Vietnam, I visited a Catholic orphanage near the Marble Mountain Air Facility in Danang several times to interact with the Amerasian children—children fathered by American military servicemen to Vietnamese mothers and then abandoned and shunned by their communities.

One day when I was still at Loyola, I spoke to Catholic Charities about adopting one or two of these Amerasian children who were being brought into the US. That evening, I went home to tell Anna how the adoption administrators had said our case was very favorable. I was excited at the thought of finally starting our family, and it meant so much to me to support some of these innocent children who were suffering so unjustly. I'd had such a difficult childhood that I longed to provide a loving home to a little one in similarly tough circumstances.

But Anna's response was more than startling.

"Dave, the truth is—I don't want to adopt a child. In fact, I never wanted to have children at all."

Anna had been adopted, and we had talked about having children earlier in our marriage, so this utterance was completely out of the blue. A total surprise. I had a visceral reaction deep in my gut to her pronouncement. This was the moment our own marriage began to disintegrate. By the time Diane had separated from Steve in 1977, Anna and I had finalized our divorce.

Reunited, eleven years later

Once Diane and I were both single again, our good friends Tom and Tracy played matchmakers—they were determined that we should get together. Tom and Tracy knew how much I loved children and how that issue had contributed to my divorce. They also figured that since I was a toxicologist and Diane was a nurse, we'd have some mutual compatibility on that level as well.

Diane wasn't that interested in a new relationship—she had just given birth to Katie a few months earlier, and her primary concern was taking care of her young children. But I called her anyway. The first time I called to talk about something other than a toxicology report on one of her patients, we chatted for over an hour. After that, she could see how much we had in common and that perhaps getting to know me might not be such a bad idea after all.

The next time I called, we talked for several hours, which eventually led me to ask her out on a date. Our originally scheduled date, however, was postponed when my beloved grandfather Lee Black had another heart attack, and I traveled back to Michigan to see him, which turned out to be the last time before he passed away. He had been a quiet but strong role model for me as a child, and he would revisit me in a special way in the future.

My first date with Diane was the only date we would have alone (except for several trips we would take) until all three children went off to college. It was Sunday, July 16, 1978— just shy of eleven years since the time she'd first caught my attention at the Andover Homecoming dance. Diane farmed out the children for the evening: a friend took Steve, who was six at the time; her sister, Pattie, took Jill, who was three; and another friend watched Katie, who was just a few months old.

I drove us down to Washington, DC, so we could spend the afternoon visiting museums along the National Mall and then have dinner that evening. The day was beautiful and warm. We toured the Museum of Natural History, the Museum of American History, and then the Air and Space Museum.

At the time, the Museum of American History was still called the Museum of History and Technology. I had been there before with a neighbor of my former in-laws, a really great guy named Hartley, whom we called "Smokie," and our wives. I particularly remembered an exhibit of farm implements from the eighteenth and nineteenth centuries. Smokie was a decade a two older than I was and had been raised on a farm, and we had spent hours figuring out how every one of those tools worked. When Diane and I went through the same exhibit during our date, I explained to her what I'd learned about those tools from Smokie. We also saw an eighteenth century house that had been built with wooden pegs rather than nails. That may sound dull to the average person, but Diane had an aptitude for mechanical things, and she was just as interested in this classic engineering as I was.

In fact, Diane was interested in a wide variety of topics. I knew from our conversations that I could talk to her about most any issue. We seemed to have all the same values. We both felt optimistic about the future, regardless of our recent circumstances. I don't think I was trying to impress her, but I loved children, so I also asked her more about Steve, Jill, and Katie. We talked like we really knew each other—it all felt very natural.

That evening, we walked along the sidewalk in front of the Air and Space Museum to head over to dinner at Hogates, a landmark seafood restaurant. I'm the romantic in the family—Diane swears she doesn't remember me from the Homecoming dance, and she probably doesn't remember the restaurant on our first date either! I not only remember it, but I also remember eating the grouper stuffed with crab and some of Hogate's famous rum buns.

On our way home, we stopped to pick up each of the children, ending at Diane's house where her sister, Pattie, was waiting with Jill. When we pulled up, I got to the front door first. Inside, there was Jill, this beautiful blond, blue-eyed three-year-old.

She looked at me and said, "Are you going to be my new daddy?"

I cannot recall if I said anything in response since I was so surprised. I don't think that is the common ending to a first-time date! I have a wonderful recollection of her pretty little face looking up at me and how sweet she was.

There was little doubt about whether Diane and I would have a good time on that first date, but the future was uncertain. She wanted to keep things friendly, and I hadn't ever dated a woman with children before. But we certainly enjoyed the dinner and conversation, and we were both confident by the end of the evening that we would see each other again.

And of course we did. The next time I saw Diane, she was lying in the street under a jacked-up old Chrysler, attempting to remove a rusty muffler. When I said that she was mechanically inclined, I really wasn't kidding.

It was our second date, and we planned to enjoy a backyard barbecue with the children. When I drove up, I was tickled to see her underneath her car—this was uncharacteristic of any woman I had known before. I wondered how in the world she knew what she was doing. I had grown up working in gas stations and I knew a lot about cars, so I crawled underneath the car to help her out.

Diane's car was a white, six-cylinder Chrysler that was probably ten or eleven years old by then. In northern states that have snowy winters, the road salt can cause a lot of damage to a car's undercarriage. The metal along her car's exhaust system was badly rusted. Diane had succeeded at disconnecting the old muffler from the tailpipe, but we had to get it the rest of the way off without damaging the exhaust pipe. Using tricks I learned changing mufflers in the gas station when I was young, we were able to completely remove the rusted out muffler and install a new one.

After we finished putting on the new muffler, we crawled out and let the car down.

Diane looked at me and said, "Next weekend, I want you to show me how to tune the car."

And the next weekend, that's just what we did. This was back when it was not too unusual to have a dwell meter and a timing light, and you could change the capacitor and ignition points yourself. This woman has always been fearless in terms of taking on a challenge and fixing what's broken.

One time long after we were married, I came home to find the washing machine upside down and Diane working to fix the motor. Later on, when we were living in Hendersonville, we had been talking about opening up a wall between two living areas to create more space. Again, I came home from work and found she'd taken a hammer and knocked out most of the wall until it was a wide, open arch. Diane knows how to get a job done. Her independence and mechanical inclinations have always been attractive characteristics to me.

During that second date, after we had fixed her muffler, we cooked hamburgers on an old charcoal grill lit up by lighter fluid. Later that night, Diane joked that we should go over to her mom and dad's house and beat on the windows. "Joe and Debbie and Pattie and Oats are sleeping over so they can go crabbing early in the morning," she said. "Let's go harass them."

Joe was her oldest brother, and Debbie was his wife. I had met her sister, Pattie, but that name Oats really rung a bell. *Where have I heard that name before?* It finally dawned on me that Oats was the boy at the gas station Anna wanted to visit before the Homecoming dance back in 1967. Now Oats was dating Diane's sister, Pattie, and eventually we would be brothers-in-law and he would become a great friend.

"Will you marry me?"

I hadn't dated much before I married Anna, but after we divorced, I found myself dating not just one nurse but three. Let's just say I was a bit of a late bloomer. Keeping my schedule straight took quite a bit of effort. Given my active social life, I wasn't too serious about my doctoral work. When I wasn't out on the town, I was working extra shifts in the pathology lab to help pay for it all. Diane didn't know about the other two women I had been seeing, but in the end it wouldn't matter.

By the fourth date, I knew that this very independent lady was the woman for me.

In January of 1979, Diane and I took a trip to the Killington Mountain Resort in Vermont. Although we had been together less than a year—and I hadn't yet bought a ring—this would be the trip when I'd ask her to marry me. I had not only fallen in love with her, but her children had dug their way into my heart as well. I had also met and grown fond of both her parents. We hadn't really talked about marriage, but we had been dating exclusively, and it felt so comfortable and natural that I knew this was my family. I knew that Diane was the right person to spend my life with. I thought I just needed to find the right moment to make it official.

That moment materialized as we were riding a ski lift in windy, frigid weather. It was cold as anything I remembered from Michigan winters on that ride—I swear it must have been minus fifteen degrees. Diane and I were snuggled together under a stiff and frozen blanket, trying to keep warm and shivering all the way to the top of the slope.

I leaned my nearly frozen face closer to hers and asked, "Diane, will you marry me?"

Just a simple, direct request. I had no fear about how she would respond. And I don't think she was all that surprised either.

She smiled and said, "Yes!"

And then we sealed the proposal with a kiss. We knew we were meant for each other. I was thrilled to start a new life with Diane. There was so much we had in common, and of course I loved the children dearly.

While Diane and I were dating, I had a townhouse in Towson on the north side of Baltimore that Anna and I had owned but which I had purchased from her during our divorce. After Diane and I were engaged, we decided to consolidate—though consolidating wasn't much of a choice since we were both struggling financially. I rented out the townhouse and moved my belongings into Diane's basement during a weekend when Steve had the two older children. I was in the basement sorting and arranging my things when they finally came home.

Little Steve, who was about seven, walked down the stairs and looked around at all the new furniture.

"Wow, we're fixing up the basement!" he said. "This looks pretty nice."

Jill, who was only four, came down a little later after Steve. She looked around and came up with quite a different conclusion.

"That's Mr. Dave's couch. That's Mr. Dave's chair. Hey, Mr. Dave's moved in!"

I laughed at how tuned in she was to what was going on. It was a classic moment showing the difference between boys and girls. And as it turned out, I was going to be Jill's new daddy after all.

CHAPTER 3

THE POLAROID FAMILY

Though it only took us six months to get engaged, it would take more than a year before Diane and I would be able to be married. After she and Steve separated, Diane had retained an attorney, although in the state of Maryland, couples had to wait a year before obtaining a divorce. Her attorney wasn't doing much of anything besides taking her money, and when he did send notices and papers, Steve wouldn't respond.

Once we were engaged, I told her I wanted to try something different.

I retained a friend named Shawn Alcarese to take over the divorce proceedings. Shawn proved to be an aggressive family attorney—he got the paperwork rolling and even hired couriers to personally serve Steve the necessary documents to sign.

At one point during the divorce proceedings, Shawn brought up the fact that Steve owed about $9,000 in back child support.

"I'm not worried about that," I told him.

"No, Dave, we should see what we can get for this," Shawn responded. "How about I tell Steve that you and Diane will forgive the back child support in exchange for his parental rights?"

"What? He won't do that. There's no way he's going to give up these beautiful children for adoption for money."

For a while after their parents' divorce, young Steve and Jill had weekend visits and other contact with their biological father. Big Steve chose to believe the baby, Katie, wasn't even his child, despite the fact that she has her father's coloring and features. Regardless, I couldn't imagine him giving up the children.

"Dave, it doesn't hurt to ask," said Shawn.

And Shawn was right after all. Steve agreed to give the children up for adoption—for the money.

I had gone bass fishing with Steve and Tom a number of times. Steve worked as an accountant for Bethlehem Steel in Dundalk, Maryland, and I assumed he was doing fine financially. But on those trips, Steve talked about money more than anything. He seemed obsessed with accumulating lots of cash. So perhaps I shouldn't have been surprised by his decision, but these were three beautiful, wonderful children. It was breathtaking and troubling that a parent would do such a thing.

At the same time, I have to admit this turned out great for our family. It certainly simplified our lives and removed a lot of potential conflict and relationship difficulties. Even before

Diane's divorce was final, we initiated the process for me to adopt the children.

Not long into our marriage, we had an ugly moment with young Steve who became very angry with us, believing that Diane and I were keeping his father from seeing him. We did our best to calm him and tell him how much we loved him. We couldn't tell him that his father had given up all visitation rights—that he hadn't even expressed a desire for visitation. Though this relieved us of a lot of complications, the separation was certainly hard on the children. They never saw Steve's face again for the rest of their lives.

Years later, when Jill and Katie were young college students down in Florida, they managed to track Steve down and get him on the phone. Katie never knew him as a child, and Jill's memories were vague. The girls didn't relate specifically what happened during that conversation for another year afterward, but we learned that whatever Steve said to them left them shaken and in tears.

Steve had gone to a dark place and never came out of it. He ended up drinking himself to death in September of 2004, when he was only fifty-five years old. I was probably more upset than the rest of the family—I used to go fishing with him and knew him. After he and Diane broke up, he married several more times and had other children—half siblings my children have never known.

And they truly are my children now. The Maryland Department of Human Services approved the adoption a week before Diane and I were married—I was a father before I was Diane's husband. Diane has always joked that she should have taken advantage of that and gotten out of town because they were my children at that point!

A "Cozy" wedding

Our wedding day was Friday, June 13, 1980, just shy of two years since our first date. Though we knew we wanted a small wedding, we still wanted to find a way to make it special. My best man, Bernie, told us about Eyler's Valley Chapel near Thurmont, which is about sixty miles from Ferndale. Built in 1857, the little stone church is nestled in a wooded area near Catoctin Mountain Park. It has an all-wooden interior—and no electricity. To this day, the chapel is lit by seventy-two candles instead.

When we met with the pastor about our wedding service, he recommended the nearby Cozy Country Inn & Restaurant for our dinner reception and weekend accommodations.

I worked the Friday we were married, leaving the lab early enough to pick up Diane and the children, who were eight, five, and two by that point. Our wedding party was intimate—Diane's parents, Pattie and Oats, Tom and Tracy, and my best man Bernie and his wife, Becky.

For the ceremony, Diane wore a simple flowered sundress, and I wore the only suit I owned. We were married around sundown, and as the sun dipped below the horizon, the light grew dim inside the church. Burning candles cast light and shadows as we finally said, "I do." A moment after I had kissed my bride, the church bell started ringing. We looked over to see Oats holding Katie in the bell tower, pulling the rope that rang the big church bell.

We stayed in the church chatting for a few minutes and then traveled over to the Cozy Restaurant. The dinner we served our family and friends was modest but tasty, complete with a beautiful two-tier wedding cake.

Diane and I were very much in love, but also very strapped for cash. In those days, we didn't have two nickels to rub together, so there was nothing fancy about this wedding. I still have the receipt for the marriage license we secured from the clerk of the Circuit Court of Frederick County— the license cost $2. We got our wedding rings at Best Buy for less than $150. Our "honeymoon suite," if you could call it that, at the Cozy Inn cost $19.43 per night, which was pretty cheap even by 1980 rates.

After dinner, Pattie and Oats took the children to go back to Baltimore, and our guests headed home. Diane and I spent the rest of the weekend at the nearby Cunningham Falls State Park. It was a beautiful, sunny weekend, and we went canoeing on the lake and walked wooded trails. We even went to a yard sale and bought a bunch of junk—a toaster, toys, an unopened set of beer glasses, a unicycle for Steve. The toaster lasted quite a few years. Steve never quite conquered the unicycle, and I think we still have the beer glasses we bought!

Diane and I only ever had one date alone—and our weekend in Frederick County would be the only honeymoon we enjoyed until all the children had finally gone off to college!

The Polaroid family

Diane and I drove back to Ferndale the Sunday after our wedding, which happened to be Father's Day. I had gotten married and become a father to three children pretty much all at once—I liked to call this my "Polaroid family."

Our lives were busy right from the start. Though I had lost my focus on the doctorate, Diane helped me get back on track. I worked at Maryland Medical Laboratory during the day, so my routine was to come home and have dinner with the family, and then while Diane got the kids ready for bed, I would leave to conduct my research at the medical examiner's office in downtown Baltimore. Sometimes after dinner, the children would lock the doors so I couldn't leave. We had this game where they wrapped themselves around my legs in an effort to keep me home. Once I had to jump a fence, and I ripped my pants at the seat and had to go back inside to get dressed all over again!

At the laboratory, I usually performed experiments until about midnight. Working alone in the medical examiner's building was an interesting experience. The elevators would go up and down between the floors, the doors would open, but no one would be there. As the only one normally working in the building at night, and knowing the autopsy room was storing the recently deceased until fully examined for cause of death, it created quite a macabre research experience!

Back at home after midnight, I often took Katie out of her crib to play for a while, and then she'd go right back to sleep. We crawled around on the floor together and underneath and around the furniture. It was great fun. I went to bed around two in the morning, got up at six, and then started the day all over again.

After we were married, Diane cut down her nursing shifts to just the weekends so she could be with the children during the workweek. From home, she created a number of small businesses, such as baking and decorating beautiful cakes for friends and family for special occasions like Mother's Day or Valentine's Day. She had a great talent for it—these cakes were truly works of art. At the same time, she sold Mary Kay cosmetics as an incorporated independent business. At one point, Diane opened a licensed daycare business in our little house that she managed for several years—she took care of not only our three children but also another six or seven children. Though her background was in nursing, her ventures taught her essential business skills, like how to balance a budget, invest, hire employees, and grow a company. She is definitely a multitasker!

Typically when you get married, there's a lot you don't know about your spouse because you haven't lived together day in and day out for long. But Diane and I started off with three children, which revealed a lot about each of us to the other: I knew immediately what kind of mother she was, and she immediately saw what kind of father I was. One of the things I naively thought when I married Diane was that all I had to do was love these three children and everything would be just fine. I had an instant family, and I didn't really understand all that was going to come of the arrangement. To Diane's credit, she handled the challenges that arose far better than I did at times.

I mentioned young Steve's anger over his absent biological father, but that was only the start of our trials with him. I learned from Diane that when Steve was only three years old he put an extension cord in his mouth—an incident that nearly killed him. That day, Diane was in her kitchen scrubbing the floor when she realized her young son had been quiet for too long. When he didn't respond to her calls, she rushed out and found him lying under the Christmas tree, unresponsive and not breathing. Apparently he had put his mouth on the part where the end of one cord plugged into the extension of another. The saliva that dripped into the connection caused an electric shock. The shock burned out part of his mouth, which had to be surgically repaired. Though the scars aren't visible today, he had to have multiple operations that left him with a lasting fear of needles and doctors.

When Diane found him, she immediately resuscitated him and rushed him to the ER at St. Agnes Hospital where she worked. It still amazes me to imagine how quickly and professionally she must have reacted to save her child. Diane has shared with me how this scared her to death. Steve only stayed one night in the hospital, but in addition to the operations to fix his mouth, he later had to have speech therapy.

In addition to this accident, Steve had significant learning disabilities growing up. He couldn't see or hear the difference between vowel sounds and the letters B, D, and P. Besides these dysfunctions, he had severe attention deficit disorder and was struggling in school. Being a Marine, I thought it was an issue of discipline and lack of focus on his part. His school wanted him put on medication, but we were both adamantly opposed to any drug administration. All of the proposed solutions to the problem were what were standard and mainstream at the time, but Diane rejected all of it and said, "No, there's a better answer." She was determined to figure out what was behind Steve's struggles.

Diane kept searching and researching and asking questions. We struggled for quite a while with Steve's issues in school before she finally discovered the Feingold diet, a nutritional program developed by pediatric allergist Dr. Ben Feingold that eliminates foods whose additives were thought to affect individuals' behavior and learning ability. As a toxicologist, I originally dismissed the diet as unlikely to be the solution to the problem. These substances are basically inorganic molecules, not like the chemicals contained in pharmaceutical drugs that interact with bioreceptors and affect behavior. But

Diane insisted that we try the diet and see if had a positive impact on Steve's disabilities.

As it turned out, Steve really was very sensitive to processed and preserved foods and candies like M&Ms—anything with certain colorings, flavorings, and other additives. We immediately began to see a huge improvement in his behavior. By the time we discovered this dietary intervention, Steve was ten years old and several grade levels behind his classmates. We had been trying to work with the public school system to manage his various issues, but we ended up placing him in a private setting instead.

The Harbor School in Annapolis was founded by an innovative educator named Dr. Linda Jacobs to provide individualized education for those with learning challenges. She had different methods and approaches that were more attuned to a particular child's needs. If a child could learn better sitting under the desk than at the desk, she would allow him or her to do so. At the Harbor School, Steve advanced several grade levels in one year. He had been tagged and typed as a bad kid when he wasn't—he just couldn't keep up due to his sensitivity to food additives combined with his speech, auditory, and visual deficits. It was a remarkable transformation, and it all came about because Diane is the kind of person who addresses challenges straightforwardly and looks for unorthodox solutions. Her determination without a doubt made a huge difference in Steve's educational outcome and also his self-image. Children with learning disabilities are often typed as problem children, as opposed to discovering what the real reasons may be for their difficulties. Ultimately the whole family ended up on the Feingold diet. We raised and harvested our own fruits and vegetables, some of which we froze or canned for the winter. We bought meat directly from farmers so it wasn't processed. And Diane baked all the bread. We were healthy before healthy was fashionable. Diane was so passionate about the results from the Feingold diet that she became an advocate—she spoke to local families and schools about the impact of food additives on education and the benefits of the program. This is just what happens when Diane becomes involved in an important issue—she ultimately takes a leadership position to leverage her knowledge for greater benefit.

And Steve turned out great. After high school, he joined the Navy and served during Operation Desert Storm, and he later obtained an associate's degree in fire sciences. Today he works successfully in facilities development and management.

Despite these challenges, we had a happy family life, and the children brought us so much joy. One episode that makes me laugh happened when Diane and I were working together to renovate the bathroom in our little house on Ferndale Ave., while our three children and their cousin Chad were playing in the backyard.

One of the children walked into the house, and each step left a black footprint on the floor. Whether it was Steve or Chad I no longer remember, but I do remember I simply picked him up and carried him back outside. That's when I saw the children had taken the black charcoal out of the little grill we had in the backyard and had thrown it into the kiddie pool that they were playing in. As I washed off one child with water from the garden hose, another child ran into the house and added another set of black tracks across the floor. So I darted after that one to bring him or her back outside. It was a merry-go-round—as soon as I washed and cleaned one child, another dirty one ran inside. I started laughing so hard I couldn't control myself, and I had to call Diane for help. Eventually we trapped them all outside and hosed them down.

There were many fun moments like this, and we cherished every one of them.

A woman of deep faith

One of Diane's qualities that was not fully revealed until after we were married was the depth of her Christian faith. While we were dating, we talked very little about God and much more about family and our hopes for the future, like our shared dream of eventually living in a rural setting and making use of the land. In all candor, I had no idea what a strong woman of faith she was. As far as I could tell, the woman I dated didn't go to church—though in hindsight, it was because she worked on Sundays. But the woman I married did, especially once I was there to help with the children. As a single working mom of three little ones, she couldn't get to church the way she had as a younger person. Once we were married, she was anxious to resume going to church every Sunday.

At the time, I had no faith of my own. I wouldn't say I was an atheist—more like agnostic or perhaps more honestly just spiritually lazy. As a child, I briefly belonged to a Boy Scout troop that had met in a church. And when I was very young, my mother was a Christian Scientist and took me a few times to her church, but I hadn't been raised in the church like Diane. I tell people I survived the Vietnam War and a Jesuit education without ever finding my faith, which requires some serious indifference.

Every Sunday, Diane took the children to church and Sunday school without me. It wasn't necessarily a point of stress between us until the children started asking why Daddy wasn't going to church. Their pointed comments about my failure to attend spurred me to finally start joining the family on Sundays, but I was very uncomfortable.

I observed over those years how Diane continued to grow spiritually and how much her faith continued to deepen. Without a doubt, her commitment to her faith deeply inspired my own faith journey. As it turned out, my personal conversion experience happened in a dream—I tell people I slept through my mountaintop experience.

Since my father was absent or abusive most of my upbringing, the only male role model I had besides John Wayne was my paternal grandfather, Lee Black. He had come to faith in Christ right before he died. One night when I was about thirty-six, I had a very vivid dream that I had died and was waiting in a room on the threshold of heaven. I waited and waited, and then my beloved grandfather came into the room to visit me. It was like he was right there in real life. He told me how much he missed me and loved me, and then he crossed back over the threshold—but I couldn't go with him.

When I woke up the dream was almost overpowering, and I said, "I want to be able to go with him and where he went."

And that's what caused me to start thinking more deeply about matters of the spirit. I began to take baby steps on a journey that continues to this day—and Diane has been a big part of that journey by sharing her faith and offering her patience.

For several years into our marriage, our family continued to live in the same small house near Diane's parents—not more than fifteen hundred square feet, a partially finished attic, and no air-conditioning . In warm seasons, whenever we sat together in the living room to watch television, we would sweat buckets and hope for a breeze to come through the open windows. Besides the heat, we were really cramped for space. I don't know how Joe and Audrey raised four children in a house similarly small, but we needed something bigger.

While in search of another home, we stumbled across a new community in development near Annapolis, about twenty-five minutes from our home in Ferndale. We loved the efficient layouts and soon put a contract to build a new home of our own. Diane visited the building site on a regular basis, taking the workers homemade cakes and cookies, and occasionally I'd bring beer and pizza on a Friday afternoon. The extra kindness to the builders and subcontractors helped—the workers added extra touches, and the house turned out great, and we looked forward to the next chapter of our life together.

I finished my doctorate in the spring of 1983—nine years after I started. We had a celebration in the backyard of our Ferndale home and moved a week later into the new house on Kings College Drive. I stayed on at Maryland Medical Laboratory where I had been working full-time while earning my degree. I had worked there performing toxicology testing for overdoses, employee drug testing, and drug counseling testing.

In that era, Diane worked in home health care nursing, and in 1985, she started a master's program in pastoral counseling at Loyola University, where I'd completed my undergraduate studies. We had been attending a church that was developing a program for comprehensive health care for its congregants and community, which would include counseling. The pastor approached Diane and asked her to consider getting a degree that would allow her to provide pastoral counseling as part of that program. As a nurse, she already had an affinity for taking care of people, but she would be able to do more than just treat the body—she would treat the soul as well. She has always been concerned not only with people's physical health but also their emotional and psychological well-being.

As a pastoral counselor, she hoped to work with elderly congregants within the church, advising them on medications and treatments and acting as a liaison between them and their doctors. She envisioned holistic care where the spiritual component became an extension of her nursing practice. This was one of the ways I witnessed her faith deepen and grow, and I found it very inspiring. This is a woman who could have been a doctor or a pastor. The counseling program was important to her, and I was entirely supportive.

We had been settled into our lives on Kings College Drive for several years when I got a call at work that would change the course of my career and our family's future. Little did I know back then that this next move would also set a new course for Diane's life that would lead us both to places we never could have imagined.

CHAPTER 4

THAT'S THE SOUTH

Three years after Diane and I had moved our family into the new home on Kings College Drive, I received a phone call from Nashville, Tennessee, that indicated our lives might be about to change.

I had been a longtime employee at Maryland Medical Laboratory, which was founded by pathologist Selvin Passen, MD, during the time I was serving in Vietnam. Since then, he had grown the laboratory to about fifty laboratory professionals. Eventually Maryland Medical would employ about two thousand scientists and support staff. Not long after I completed my doctorate, Selvin decided he wanted all of his MDs and PhDs on contract. The process of negotiating a long-term contract took us many months.

On Tuesday, January 28, 1986—which was both my birthday and the day of the space shuttle Challenger disaster—I had stayed late to meet with Selvin and finally sign our long-negotiated employment agreement. About ten minutes ahead of our meeting, I received a phone call from Dr. Fred Gorstein at Vanderbilt University.

"We got your name from the Academy of Forensic Sciences," said Dr. Gorstein. "We've been searching for a doctorate to set up a new drug testing program here."

Unbeknownst to me, Vanderbilt had an anabolic steroid scandal, and they were looking to establish a new laboratory to test athletes for the use of performance-enhancing drugs. He asked me if I'd be interested in interviewing for a professorship.

"Dr. Gorstein, this is pretty awkward because I'm getting ready to walk in and sign a multiyear agreement with my current employer."

"Please don't do that, Dr. Black. Would you at least come to Vanderbilt and meet with us? You've received such great recommendations."

I told him I would think about it. After I hung up, I walked into Selvin's office.

"You're not going to believe this," I said, "but I just got this phone call . . . "

We had been negotiating the contract for about eight or nine months at that point. To his credit, Selvin didn't get upset.

"Dave, I don't want you to sign this agreement if you'll regret it. I want you to go to Vanderbilt and see what they have to offer."

My first interview was scheduled for the second week of February. I flew out of Baltimore in a snowstorm, and when I landed in Nashville, the forsythias were blooming, and the dogwoods were also showing their blossoms and color. Tennessee was having an early spring, and it was beautiful. It felt like a sign.

After half a day of interviews, I called Diane that night from the hotel.

"Honey, this may be something worthwhile for us to think about," I told her.

The thought of moving was difficult for us both, though the job presented a worthwhile opportunity and seemed like a risk worth taking.

After another day of interviews that ended up running late, Fred Gorstein took me to the airport in heavy traffic, and I ended up missing my flight home. That flight happened to be the last flight to Baltimore, so my only other option was a flight to DC instead. This was 1986—before cellphones and instant communication were common. I had no way to get a hold of Diane and let her know I'd missed the flight and changed my travel plans. She would be waiting in Baltimore with no idea my flight had changed.

When I finally arrived at Washington National, the airport was closing down for the night, and there were no taxis waiting at the curb. I knew Diane would be very concerned, wondering where I was. I ended up in the lost luggage area of the airport, amidst mountains of bags and suitcases, and talked the service person into taking me with him when he drove lost luggage to their owners in Baltimore.

After being treated like a VIP by Vanderbilt, here I was in the back of a lost luggage van trying to get home!

Needless to say, Diane was upset but relieved when I finally found my way to our home in Annapolis.

In many ways, that trying start to this potential transition represented just how difficult this decision was going to be. We had this new house we loved on Kings College Drive—and a new backyard deck we took two summers to build. Diane was close to her parents, Joe and Audrey, and the children loved their grandparents and were used to being with them every weekend. We usually ate steamed crab with her parents and Pattie and Oats every Saturday night and then played cards. Leaving them would be very painful not only for the children but also for Diane and me. Then there was her pastoral counseling program to consider. She had already completed two years of classes and had only her practicum to complete when we were faced with this move.

Diane prayed a great deal about it over the months I continued to fly back to Nashville for additional interviews. She joined me during my third trip because Vanderbilt wanted to show us around and assist us in looking for a new home. Our escorts took us to areas such as Belle Meade and Green Hills to show us potential homes.

After looking at the homes and the prices in these areas, Diane cried all the way back to the hotel. The neighborhoods they'd shown us were entirely outside of our budget. Considering the salary we were being offered, we didn't see how we could afford to live in Nashville. We also had trouble finding a Lutheran church for our family, which was important to Diane. We returned to Maryland discouraged about where we would settle in Tennessee.

Ultimately we agreed that I would take the position, which I finally confirmed to Vanderbilt around the month of May, but we still needed to find a place to live. Some friends of ours from church heard we were struggling with what to do.

"We have family in Hendersonville," they said. "Let us call them and see if they know of anyone who can help you."

And this is how we came to meet Andy Barrett, a man who has been a gift from God to our family on numerous occasions.

While I was transferring responsibilities and wrapping up loose ends at Maryland Medical Laboratory, Diane flew back to Tennessee on her own to meet with Andy, our new real estate agent. After Andy showed her around Hendersonville, Diane found a newly built house that she liked, and they put a contract on it right away. I hadn't seen the house, but I completely trusted her judgment, and I knew what a relief it was to have a home we could afford.

A few months later, on Friday, June 27, 1986, we were packed and ready to start our long drive and journey to Hendersonville. Diane had taken care of almost every aspect of arranging our relocation with the moving company since I had worked almost to the last day at Maryland Medical completing the transition of my duties. We had a buyer on our house on Kings College Drive, but that afternoon, we found out our attorneys hadn't yet filed all the necessary paperwork—which meant we would not have the money to buy the house in Hendersonville on the following Monday morning. We didn't know what we were going to do, but Andy insisted we come anyway.

We left that night. I took Steve, Katie, our dog, and our pet bird in our Suburban, which was hitched to a camper filled with many of our belongings. Diane drove our little Ford Escort with our cat and daughter Jill, who cried the entire way to Tennessee. Of all the children, Jill was the most upset to leave her friends behind. She was also upset about moving to Tennessee, where her friends told her only dumb hillbillies lived.

The moving truck was set to meet us at our new house that next Tuesday. The trip took us two long and stressful days, and then once we finally arrived on Sunday, Diane couldn't find the house! We needed to drop off the camper and figure out what we would do the next day to purchase our house. There we were—a Suburban pulling a camper, the Escort and all the pets and worn-out children, driving up and down neighborhood streets looking for a house I had never even seen. Though we finally found the house, it wasn't like we could stay there that night anyway. We checked into a really cheap motel instead, which was the only motel in Hendersonville. The kids were still upset, and by then Diane was upset too. This wasn't the greatest start to our new adventure. When Diane pulled back the covers on her bed in the motel, she found a dead cockroach—that pretty much summed up the whole trip over from Maryland.

Monday morning I met Andy Barrett for the first time.

"Mr. Barrett, you don't know me," I began, "but as Diane warned you, we didn't sell our home back in Maryland this past Friday, and I don't have the money to buy this house this morning."

"Dr. Black, we're going to buy this house today."

Then Andy proceeded to write a personal check for $30,000 so we could make a down payment on the home. I am still amazed at what Andy did that day.

When I asked him for something to sign, he simply replied, "No, we'll do it on a handshake."

So I shook Andy's hand—a man I'd known for about five minutes—and Diane and I had our first house in Tennessee. When the sale of our house in Maryland closed several weeks later, I told Andy I wanted to pay interest on the loan, but he refused to accept my offer.

This act of extravagant generosity and hospitality was our introduction to Tennessee and our new community. And it goes without saying that Andy became a dear friend of the family.

That's the South

When Diane told her friends we were headed to Tennessee, their response was, "That's the South!" Our daughter Jill's preteen friends teased her that she was going to become a hillbilly. Tennessee didn't have the best image back in Maryland.

When I was growing up in Michigan, there were a lot of residents from Tennessee and Kentucky who had arrived during the Great Depression to find work and then *en masse* during World War II to make tanks and planes. The kids I grew up with were the children of these transplants. When we arrived in Tennessee in 1986, the culture, customs, and friendliness of the region reminded me of what I had known as a child.

Diane, however, had had no such experience; she had never lived outside of Maryland. She didn't know what it was like to see everyone wave at you, whether they knew you or not. She hadn't gone to check out at a grocery store or retail store and had the cashier start chatting. Back in Maryland, folks you didn't know rarely made eye contact, let alone struck up a conversation easily. The friendliness in Tennessee made such a positive difference to us both, and we immediately felt at home.

Over the next few days, as we unloaded the moving truck and unpacked our boxes, neighbors from up and down our street came by to say hello and welcome us to the neighborhood. Several of the new neighbors we met that first week in Hendersonville have become lifelong friends to this day. One couple, Barb and Harry, had moved into the area from Indiana not long before we did. They had three children about the same ages as ours, and we all bonded right from the start. Cathy and Don were another pair who had moved to the neighborhood from Michigan and became close friends of our family.

The Fourth of July was that Friday, and our next-door neighbors, Ralph and Karen, invited us to join the party. Ralph and Karen were also in the process of moving in, and their washing machine and clothes dryer were sitting on their front lawn. These people were artistic and creative, so they decided to throw a hillbilly party and play up the funniest Southern stereotypes. They stuck a jacked-up car in their front yard alongside the washer and dryer. Diane and I went out and purchased bib overalls and trucker caps and dressed the part of true Southerners. Ralph and Karen's family even put on a comedy show in their garage.

The Thursday before the party, I stayed up all night with the guys from the neighborhood doing a pig roast over an open fire in the yard. I'd never done a pig roast in my life! Any lingering doubts about our decision to move soon evaporated as we embraced our new life in Tennessee.

I officially started my job at the Vanderbilt Drug Testing Laboratory on July 1, 1986. The new position was a financial step up from where I had been, not to mention we paid much less in property taxes in Tennessee than we had back in Maryland and could purchase a much better home on a bigger piece of property. And we soon learned that Tennessee had no state income tax, which was a big difference from our tax burden back in Maryland. As a result, Diane could spend more time with the children. She worked PRN for the emergency room at Hendersonville Hospital (now called the Hendersonville Medical Center), mostly because she loved nursing.

One of the things we loved when we came to Tennessee was how doctors often prayed with patients before surgery or another kind of treatment. We found that to be comforting in an unexpected way. Diane had hoped to be part of that approach to patient care, but she'd had to drop out of her pastoral counseling program at Loyola when we left Maryland. When I arrived at Vanderbilt, I asked Dr. Gorstein if Diane could talk to the Divinity School about resuming her counseling program there, but they wouldn't admit her unless she was pursuing a divinity degree. I was very upset and had fully expected she would be able to resume her studies at Vanderbilt.

Though we were both very disappointed, Diane didn't let this slow her down. In the fall of 1989, she was accepted into Belmont University to complete a four-year nursing degree. This is more evidence of her unstoppable determination—while working part-time and taking care of young children, she also started studying for a higher degree. She loved working in the ER and doing patient care, but she recognized that the bachelor of science in nursing (BSN) would allow her better nursing opportunities and to take on more leadership in the hospital. That's my wife: a leader in all she does.

The birth of Aegis

On January 28, 1990—my birthday again—I received a call from Dr. Gorstein for a meeting to tell me that they were withdrawing funding for my program and closing down the laboratory. The program had been successful, but Vanderbilt hadn't realized the full implications of a forensic drug-testing program. There were consequences to a positive drug test— someone lost a scholarship or received some punitive action— which is in conflict with clinical and medical care. Vanderbilt is more of a patient-centered setting where medical staff treats and cares for people compassionately, rather than hold them accountable for negative behavior.

In place of continuing to direct the laboratory, Vanderbilt offered me a service position in clinical toxicology. Although it was a generous offer, I am trained in forensics and did not want to abandon my profession. My old employer back in Maryland offered me a job if I wanted to return, but Diane and I had grown to love Tennessee, and we didn't want to leave. What's more, the children had acclimated and made friends as well. I had lived nineteen places by the time I was eighteen—I didn't want them to have the same disrupting experience growing up that I had suffered.

Rather than move out of Middle Tennessee, we decided to start our own toxicology laboratory instead. I founded Aegis Sciences Corporation with a business partner, Mark Faulkner, from Abbott Diagnostics, and three employees from the now closed laboratory at Vanderbilt. We had developed a small but growing clientele while at Vanderbilt, including colleges and national sports organizations, and we didn't want to let all that go. At the time, there were only three other toxicology laboratories in North America that were testing athletes for the possible use of performance enhancing drugs: Indianapolis,

UCLA, and Calgary, Canada. Although I perceived a strong market opportunity, the primary reason to start the business was to stay in Nashville. I really had no grand plans—I would be satisfied to just pay the bills and support my family.

I intended to grow Aegis to where it provided an adequate living—but to get there, Diane had to go back to work full-time to support our family. My salary had been cut by more than half—I didn't have the money to pay myself what Vanderbilt had been paying me. I had been consulting on various legal cases all over the world, which provided additional income, but once I was starting my own business, I wasn't able to do as much consulting as I'd been doing either. Not only that, I was now paying salaries for other people.

The company struggled at first and spent more than we were making, but I was passionate about taking care of our employees and our clients. Building Aegis was about the people and the culture we were creating, and about the people we were serving.

It was a struggle for many years with modest annual growth. The young company struggled financially as almost all small start-ups do. Diane and I had several situations where the cable or electricity was disconnected due to nonpayment—the loss of cable was always traumatic for my children, who couldn't get MTV. A few times the phone also was disconnected, and we missed a few mortgage payments. But we never missed paying a bill for the business—every invoice was paid in full and on time.

Over the next twenty-six years, Aegis would grow from an initial $70,000 loan and four staff members into a $700 million valued company and a thousand employees scattered across forty-six states.

In the beginning, however, Aegis grew very slowly. While working full time to support us, Diane endured a husband who was working eighty to a hundred hours a week. She helped me think through challenges with financing and personnel, and when I consulted on medical toxicology cases, she offered her professional knowledge. When Aegis moved from our initial location to a larger business complex, Diane came in to paint and wallpaper the walls, working shoulder to shoulder with the rest of the crew to move us in. And when we had to personally guarantee millions of dollars in debt on the company buildings and Aegis's line of credit, Diane and I both signed the papers.

Diane and I have worked as a couple to get where we are, and it's fair to say she was just as invested in the business as I was. She not only worked hard, but she took the risk and had the faith that if we worked hard, we could succeed.

When we first started Aegis, Diane was still in school at Belmont. It took her several years to finish her BSN degree. Her graduation in the spring of 1992 was memorable for several reasons—besides the great accomplishment. We also left right after the graduation ceremony to take a direct, overnight flight to London so I could testify as an expert witness for US Olympic track star Harry "Butch" Reynolds

in his legal case against the International Association of
Athletics Federations (IAAF). All the while taking care of
children and supporting an entrepreneur husband, Diane had
the tenacity and determination to finish that degree.

Diane wasn't just a working nurse and a student—she
was also an educator. In 1988, an administrator at Volunteer
State Community College in Gallatin, who knew her from
the Hendersonville Morning Rotary Club, had asked her
to fill in for a professor who at the last minute was unable
to teach the course in medical terminology. Diane was only
supposed to teach temporarily, but she ended up being the
associate professor of allied health for the next five years. Her
course in medical terminology was recorded to videotape and
used to teach college-at-home classes for several years after
she completed her appointment in 1995. Even though she
stopped teaching, Diane joined the College Foundation Board
of Trustees in 1999 and served on the board for many years.

A vicious assault

Of course, not every aspect of our life in Tennessee has
been positive. Despite the friendliness and generosity of our
region, anyone at any time might end up a victim of a violent
crime—which is just what happened to Diane one bright
summer day.

On June 29, 1994, Diane was on the Vanderbilt University
campus making arrangements for the Middle Tennessee
Lutheran Women's retreat. That afternoon, as she walked out

of the building and approached her car, she was attacked in broad daylight.

Three young black men pulled their car up to the sidewalk, and two jumped out and grabbed her. Their intention was to abduct her, but she fought back. As they yanked at her purse and grabbed her by the arms, she screamed and struggled as hard as she could. One of them punched her in the face so hard it broke her cheekbone. When they struck her face, it caused her to fall backward, hitting the concrete and injuring her back, which still causes pain all these years later.

The worst part of this attack is that it happened in broad daylight. Only one witness was nearby, a young man paralyzed with fear. Finally, someone inside the building heard Diane screaming and called the campus police. Her struggle was successful—her assailants gave up and took off with just her purse, which happened to have $1,500 in cash from the recent sale of our Jayco bunkhouse camper, money we'd intended to use for vacation. While still lying on the concrete, Diane was so close to the assailants' car that she saw the license plate and repeated the number over and over again to herself to remember it. It was a stolen plate, however, and neither the Vanderbilt campus police nor Nashville metro police were able to locate the assailants.

The official police report contained limited details of this incident, but this was a deeply traumatic event for Diane. For months afterward, whenever she encountered men who resembled her attackers, she started shaking uncontrollably.

She's since overcome that reaction, but it took several years to process the trauma. The experience made her an ardent gun-rights advocate, though she didn't get her own permit to carry until some years later.

Diane hadn't grown up around guns or weapons and hadn't previously been motivated to shoot or own a gun. However, I was accepted into a one-year Citizen FBI course, and the last meeting we had was at the firing range to shoot all the various weapons in their arsenal. I hadn't fired a weapon since I left the Marine Corps, and as I looked forward to this event, I thought it would be great for Diane. She agreed to attend, and the first weapon she fired was a fully automatic Thompson submachine gun. We stayed and fired for several hours, and Diane not only enjoyed herself but also learned she was very accurate with a handgun. Now she not only has her carry permit but is also a lifetime member of the NRA.

A heart for the community

Since our move to Tennessee, Diane had been working in the emergency room at the Hendersonville Hospital. In 1994, she was recruited to Sumner Regional Medical Center to work in outpatient surgery and recovery, and then after a few more years she became the executive director of the Sumner Regional Medical Center Foundation. As director of the Foundation, Diane established support groups for cancer patients and people with diabetes, and she conducted outreach for diabetes education. She also taught babysitting skills to young girls as part of the Foundation's community educational programs.

She was also in charge of development, including an annual fundraising gala held at either Loews Vanderbilt or Opryland. Another of her fundraising events was an annual air show at the Sumner County Regional Airport in Gallatin. One year, on a hot August day, she dressed up in an Eagle mascot costume—she'd even gone to "mascot school" ahead of the occasion. Despite her tendency to get motion sickness, she went up in one of the small planes, and then after landing, came out of the plane to greet the crowd of spectators. She got entirely overheated and sick, and we had to get her into the air-conditioned terminal to recuperate! Even though she had a pretty good idea the plane ride would make her nauseous, she still went up to do her job and entertain the spectators.

Her fundraising events benefited the "Little House with a Heart," a house where out-of-town family members of patients receiving long-term treatment could stay. The money raised also bought hospital equipment, such as a pediatric crash cart or emergency electrocardiogram.

Diane has always had a "can-do" and "let's get it done" attitude that has defined who she is. The many local and national organizations she has worked with have discovered how determined she is and how well she works with groups of people to achieve goals. And above all else, she sets very high ethical standards for herself and those around her.

There's rarely an organization that she doesn't join without eventually becoming its leader. I think she headed almost every nonprofit in Sumner County during her early years of public service. Long before she sought public office, Diane was chairman of the Sumner County United Way, president of the Gallatin Chapter of the American Cancer Society, vice president of Habitat for Humanity of Sumner County, and a board member of the Sumner County YMCA, the American Heart Association, and other nonprofit organizations.

One of the community groups we joined together back in 1988 was the Hendersonville Rotary. The club had only recently changed its rules to allow women to join, and we were supposed to be the first husband and wife to be inducted into a Rotary Club in Tennessee—but we ended up being second. We were, however, the first husband and wife in Middle Tennessee to be inducted. It's hard to believe women were still excluded from Rotary clubs in the late 1980s, but opening up Rotary to women made a great difference to the organization. It went from being an old guys' Wednesday morning breakfast meeting to one of the most active clubs in our Rotary district. Thanks to both the inclusion of women and great leadership, Hendersonville Rotary has been Club of the Year since then, and we run about 60 projects in our community and around the world.

And, of course, Diane served as president of the Hendersonville Rotary as well—in fact, she was president when our club was named Club of the Year for our district. She was even named Rotarian of the Year in 1993.

Some of our favorite service projects were the Rotary medical missions to Guatemala. Diane helped launch the program with a Hendersonville pediatric dentist named Dr. Bill Taylor. Bill brought the project to our club, and Diane was one of the first Rotarians to volunteer for the inaugural mission trip. The initial missions focused mostly on dental work, and then we added medical and vision services later on.

We went on our first trip in 1996. At first I was opposed to these trips because I thought we had enough need in our own community—but Diane was adamant about going. I only went down because it became evident that Diane would be the only female Rotarian on the mission, and I figured I better protect my interests! During one of our first mission trips, we found a child in a village who had an open abscess in the back of his head—that child was certainly going to die. Although we were there for dentistry, we took the child back to Guatemala City to be treated by one of our Spanish physician partners, Dr. Sergio Mollinedo, at the hospital he owned.

Diane went on thirteen trips to Guatemala, and I ended up going on fifteen. I realized that when you go on these mission trips, you get back a lot more than you give. Neither of us speaks Spanish, but Diane and I love the Spanish people. We were eager to assist dentists and doctors as they treated people who had limited access to clean water, health care, education, and other means to improve themselves and their circumstances.

The Rotary Club has been just one of many organizations into which Diane has poured her heart and soul. Both of us are passionate about supporting the community in any way we can. We are both people of faith, and we believe the body of Christ is the hope of the world. We feel strongly that we're called by Christ to be servants and to lift up others in our own communities and around the world.

A vision for change

Despite our involvement with the Rotary Club and Diane's extensive community service, we didn't get very involved in political organizations until Bill Clinton was elected president. Though Diane came from a family of Democrats, she had been conservative from a young age—she was even a member of the Students for Nixon club at her high school back in Maryland. I became a staunch Republican myself during Ronald Reagan's presidency.

Two years into Clinton's first term, we began attending meetings held by the Sumner County Republican Party. We began meeting people in public office, and we even made our first donation to a local political figure. In that era, Sumner County was still rather blue—our gatherings consisted of only about a dozen people in the back of a Shoney's restaurant—but 1994 was a revolutionary year for Republicans across the country.

In the midterm elections, the GOP swept both chambers of Congress, several governorships, and hundreds of seats in state legislatures. Prior to the election, Tennessee had had a Democrat governor and two Democrat US senators, but afterward, voters had chosen Don Sundquist, a Republican, for governor, and two Republican senators, Bill Frist and Fred Thompson. Though the Tennessee General Assembly remained controlled by the Democrats, a sea change was underway.

Among our growing concerns over President Clinton's initiatives, Diane was particularly driven by serious flaws in the efforts to reform health care. In April of 1993, Tennessee governor Ned McWherter had introduced TennCare, a pilot program for state-sponsored universal coverage similar to what President Clinton was promoting on a national level. Before President Clinton's complex and expensive health-care reforms were repudiated in the fall of 1994, TennCare was already well underway.

TennCare was meant to replace the state's existing Medicaid program by consolidating a patchwork delivery system into managed care overseen by the state. The program provided health-care coverage to those who qualified for Medicaid, as well as to the uninsured and those who were uninsurable due to a preexisting medical condition. The program was conceived, approved, and implemented with unprecedented speed and with little input from key industry experts and stakeholders.

As a result, TennCare had several damaging flaws. For one, it offered a more generous benefits package than many employers offered their employees, and the ease of entry was such that people could wait until they were sick before obtaining coverage. Many businesses opted out of covering their higher-cost employees, sending them to TennCare instead and overloading the roster with very sick people. TennCare ended up covering one in four residents—a whopping 25 percent of the state's total population.

The program was easy to abuse—an audit revealed that the state ended up spending millions covering 14,000 dead enrollees, 16,500 people who lived out of state, thousands of ineligible enrollees, and even hundreds of state employees who had access to a less generous state employee insurance plan.

What's more, the tidal wave of enrollees combined with chronically low reimbursement rates to providers resulted in an unavoidable reduction in the quality of care. Even though the Tennessee legislature added $190 million to close the gap in reimbursements, many doctors and managed care companies refused to participate or dropped out of the program.[3]

By this point, Diane had spent decades as a nurse, she'd taught medical terminology at Vol State, and she'd been president of medical associations like the local chapter of the American Cancer Society. She knew firsthand how the health-care industry functioned. She understood what practices facilitated high-quality, patient-centered health care and what issues and obstacles patients and providers faced.

---

3 For a more comprehensive explanation of the issues surrounding TennCare, see "Lessons from Tennessee's Failed Health Care Reform," by Merrill Matthews, The Heritage Foundation, April 7, 2000, http://www.heritage.org/health-care-reform/report/lessons-tennessees-failed-health-care-reform.

While working as an emergency room nurse, Diane also saw firsthand the issues of misuse and overuse that arose from TennCare. She encountered people who came in with minor issues like a sore throat—despite the fact that they could have gone to a walk-in clinic or waited to see their family doctor. She would say to them, "Perhaps you don't need to be in the ER. You could go see your regular doctor tomorrow about this."

But they'd respond, "I have to work during the day tomorrow," or "I have things going on tomorrow, so I have to get seen today."

Diane believes that if patients don't have any skin in the game, then they won't make effective and efficient decisions about their health care. She also witnessed this factor in play by noticing how TennCare recipients would visit multiple doctors and receive various drugs that could interact negatively with each other. The overall result was lower quality and less cost-effective care.[4]

After only a year, massive enrollment in TennCare and out-of-control expenditures led to a state budget crisis that prompted then-governor Don Sundquist, a Republican, to propose a state income tax. I'll save that story for the next chapter—but suffice it to say that though the intentions behind the program were honorable, TennCare costs were ballooning out of control.

Although a recurring statement, I will repeat myself: Diane is a doer. She sees a problem and she decides to fix

---

4 Sterling C. Beard, "Rep. Black's healthcare prescription doesn't include the government," *The Hill*, July 30, 2012.

it—whether that's paying for nursing school, uncovering the mysterious reasons for our son's learning challenges, finding an affordable house in an unfamiliar region, or fixing a financial sinkhole before it wrecked the entire state. She is truly unstoppable when it matters. And though it would be many years before any reforms would be enacted, TennCare was what inspired her to take on her next challenge: securing a seat in the Tennessee General Assembly.

◀ Age three and already a fisherman.

Little Diane ▶ and the big catch.

Diane with brothers Doug and Joe and younger sister, Patti.
▼

◀ *Linthicum Teen Center Princess, 1967-68*

Diane and the yearbooks
▼

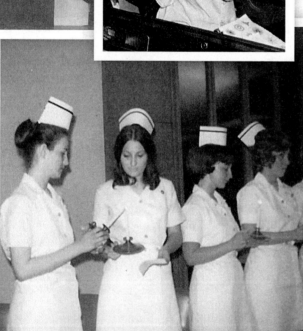

Nurse ▶
capping ceremony, 1971.

Our wedding reception ▶
at the Cozy Inn and
Restaurant,
Friday, June 13, 1980.

▲
Our annual
Christmas tree "hunt"
with family: brother-in-law Oats,
Joe, cousin Chad, and our family,
1981.

Steve, Jill, and Katie ▶
dressed up for Halloween,
1982.

Representative Randy Stamps and Diane, 1998.

In a field in Hendersonville in 1998, Diane announced she was running as a state representative candidate for the 45th State District to replace Randy Stamps.

During her 1998 ▶ campaign, Diane poses with Tommy Whittaker (left), dean of the Republican Party of Sumner County and her treasurer for all of her races, including for governor. To the right is Governor Don Sundquist who campaigned for Diane before she opposed his state income tax plan. (Gary Moor)

This political mailer, ▶ which launched the accusation that Diane had "arranged" state contracts for Aegis, was circulated during the 2008 general election in which Diane ran against Democrat Jim Hawkins. Jim is now a Republican in Sumner County and has admitted this lie was made up by the State Democrat Party. Lou Ann Zelenik has perpetuated this lie for years to attack Diane.

Diane with Wiley Sandstrom, Jon Fitzgerald, Sidney Sandstrom, and Jonathan Young.

Diane hugs our grandson Joey on the night of the 2010 primaries for the 6th Congressional District. (Samuel M. Simpkins / The Tennessean)

▲

Diane hugs our granddaughter Maddie while awaiting election results for the 6th Congressional District, 2010. (Eric Miller / Sumner A.M.)

Diane and our grandson Bear stands in front of Speaker of the House John Boehner (R-OH), as Boehner is congratulated by colleagues while entering the House following his election January 5, 2011 in Washington, DC. (Chip Somodevilla / Getty Images)

▼

◄ *Diane with Big Show at a 2015 WWE Event in Tallahassee, Florida, for grandson Easton.*

Diane with Eric Metaxas.
▼

Diane with her parents, Joe and Audrey Warren.
▼

A little older than three and still a fisherman.
▼

CHAPTER 5

THE GENERAL ASSEMBLY

Running for political office wasn't yet on Diane's mind when we initiated our involvement with the Sumner County Republican Party, but after several years of watching the state and health-care system struggle under TennCare's ballooning weight, she grew more determined to be part of the solution.

During monthly breakfast meetings with the Sumner County Republican Party, Diane and I met Rep. Randy Stamps, who served five terms as the representative for the 45th House District, which comprises Hendersonville, Gallatin, and western Sumner County. We had the chance to get to know Randy and his wife over time, and given Diane's community service, she helped him on his campaigns.

In 1998, Randy and his wife had twins, and he decided not to run for reelection. Since he was stepping down and leaving an open seat, he asked Diane to run in his place. Randy had seen her leadership in various groups where she had always been very active and frequently rose to leadership. Randy believed that she was the best potential candidate to represent the 45th House District for the Republican Party and to serve the people of Sumner County.

Given her increasing involvement in the community and local politics, Diane was cued up to receive this kind of bold invitation. As people of faith, we both decided to pray over the decision. I had grown to a point in my faith where I did indeed pray in earnest. After she announced that she would run for Randy's former seat, I often joked to people that her prayer was answered, and mine was not.

Diane was in a perfect position to take on this kind of challenge. All of the children were off to college and starting their young adult lives by this point, so she had fewer responsibilities at home and to our family. But being that involved in politics had never been a point of conversation or part of our plan. One of the things I'd always imagined was that Diane and I would be able to travel together. We were able to take a few trips when I was consulting on legal cases in various countries, and we were just waiting for the children to grow up so that we'd have more time to see the world. Politics hadn't been part of that thought process. So though I say it jokingly, I have to admit I was hesitant. Regardless of any hesitation on my part, one of the core values of our marriage has always been that we support each other in our endeavors, and Diane's fledgling political career was no exception. Diane had been key to my completing my doctorate, and it was important to support her as she began an important new chapter of her life.

Novices on the campaign trail

Diane was still the executive director for the Sumner Regional Health Systems Foundation when she ran for the Tennessee House in 1998, and she'd have to work different schedules to serve in the legislature and still function as director of the Foundation full-time. She had to ask Bill Sugg, president of Sumner Regional Health Systems from 1989 to 2009, for his support. Once he agreed, we were then free to plan and execute Diane's first campaign for public office.

In hindsight, I admit we didn't quite know what we were getting into. This was one of those decisions that had ramifications completely unknown to us. The first thing we didn't expect was that her opponent would be a young man named Charles Robert Bone, son of Charles W. Bone, one of the most influential Democrats in the state of Tennessee. Charles W. is, for example, a close friend of former vice-president Al Gore, who occasionally stayed at their home in Hendersonville.

The Bones are people of faith—in fact, we now go to church with Charles W., and he sometimes sits in the pew right behind us. I had the chance to get to know his son through the course of the campaign, and despite the differences in our political opinions, I liked him and found him to be a fine young man. Despite having a decent and likable opponent, however, we still learned firsthand just how ugly politics could be.

From the outset, friends or supporters of Diane's Democratic opponent called our house and said unflattering things directly to us. When we drove down the street, other drivers or their passengers yelled and cursed at us from their car windows. I'm confident Diane's opponent would never have supported that kind of behavior, but that's how his supporters did, in fact, behave. People get too carried away with politics. Though I have to say, if we thought *that* was bad, it was nothing like we would encounter in later campaigns.

One of the things that kept this particular campaign civil and respectful happened during the first debate between Diane and Charles Robert Bone in front of the League of Women Voters. Diane's political advisor came up with the idea to challenge Charles Robert to stay only on the issues during the campaign and forego all personal attacks. During the debate, they came to a point where Diane put this challenge before him.

"We want to run a campaign that serves the people of this county, and we need to stay on the issues," she said. "So Charles Robert, I want you to join me in a pledge that we will not attack each other's character but stick to the issues at hand."

He was so caught by surprise that he had no choice but to agree to it, and they signed that agreement right there in front of everyone. This kept the campaign very civil. It was a brilliant move because we'd never been in politics before, and Diane as a candidate didn't have to suffer what she would have had to suffer otherwise and what she would experience in future campaigns.

Diane's first campaign for a seat in the Tennessee House of Representatives was definitely a grassroots effort. That summer, she called all her close friends, and they formed what they affectionately referred to as the Kitchen Cabinet: a team of supporters and campaign volunteers who met in our kitchen to pitch in on various campaign tasks and to host rallies over hotdogs and chips in the backyard.

"We met weekly in her house to discuss strategies, who needed to run here or do this or that," said Barb. "Her energy was unbelievable. She was working a job, and yet also going out into the community to meet people and raising a great deal of money. Campaigning was a twenty-four-hour-a-day job." [5]

"We called her the Energizer Bunny," added Cathy. "She had more energy than the rest of us. Dave and I would look at each other like, 'Are you kidding me?' She had such a passion for this campaign and for making things right for other people." [6]

Campaigning for the first time was a remarkable experience. Diane had been a nurse at the Hendersonville Hospital and the Sumner County Medical Center, and she'd taught at Vol State, so we met people all over that county who knew her from one of her workplaces.

---

5 Interview with the author, December 2017.
6 Interview with the author, December 2017.

One Saturday morning, we went to a pancake breakfast and walked into a large room full of about two hundred people. From across the room, I heard a woman screaming, "Diane Black! That's Diane Black! You saved my husband's life." As it turned out, this woman's husband had arrived at the Hendersonville ER having a heart attack, and Diane had jumped up on the gurney to take care of him. The woman yelling from across the room rushed over to hug Diane and love all over her. Obviously such a spontaneous response witnessed by others would have a far bigger impact than any campaign advertisement possibly could.

There were other similar instances during the campaign. One time Diane was going around knocking on doors when she came across a man who had been working in his house when he fell and hurt himself. And there she was, a nurse, so she bandaged him and then drove him to the hospital herself.

A funny aspect of that campaign that we didn't realize would have a lasting influence was the decision to put Diane's picture on her large campaign signs, "Diane Black for State Representative." Our motivation in doing so was because there was a felon in Gallatin with the name David Black, and we figured if people saw Diane's face, they'd realize he wasn't the same David Black she's married to. People in the community knew her much better than me, but most would have realized by her picture that she was unrelated to the other David Black.

On more than one occasion, Diane walked up to a house to talk to someone and a child would answer the door.

"You're Diane Black," the child would say. "You're on the signs!"

The children were excited to recognize this woman whose face was on signs all over town. An unintended benefit of having her photo on the sign was that it became iconic in the community each election cycle. We reused those signs for every reelection afterward—later pasting a Senate sticker over it. When we finally retired them, around the time she ran for Congress, the signs had completely worn themselves out.

Given this was Diane's first foray into politics, we took a training class on how to run a campaign, which was invaluable, but we still were outspent by 50 percent. Financial support for Charles Robert's race came in from all over the United States from other influential Democrats like Senator Diane Feinstein of California. Despite the great discrepancy in fundraising, Diane won the race by about 50 percent herself: 8,471 votes to Charles Robert Bone's 5,041. She received a wonderful response throughout her campaign, and we enjoyed a great victory party. In fact, at the victory party, Charles Robert and his father came into our headquarters to personally congratulate Diane on her win. It remains one of the classiest moments we have seen in politics.

The fight against a state income tax

In January of 1999, Diane was sworn in as a freshman state representative. The race to win her first political campaign couldn't begin to compare to the challenge awaiting her during her first term in the statehouse.

That same January, Don Sundquist was sworn in for his second term as governor of Tennessee, and he then promptly announced a proposal for a state income tax to help offset the $342 million budget deficit that was quickly growing in large part due to TennCare's $4.4 billion in expenditures. Though Gov. Sundquist had previously been a staunch opponent of an income tax, he now positioned this initiative as "tax reform" and offered to lower the sales tax and tax on food to offset the added income tax. Sundquist and his supporters claimed that this new income tax was necessary to pay for education and health care—but Diane had pursued her position in the legislature for the express purpose of improving health care while reining in the runaway costs of TennCare and minimizing the size of state government. Adding an income tax was not the solution to the problem.

In an effort to garner Diane's support, Sundquist summoned her to his office and told her he needed her help on the income tax proposal.

When she refused—explaining that 83 percent of her constituency was against the tax—Gov. Sundquist told her he would not complete the long-promised Vietnam Veterans Boulevard, nor would he support her in her future reelection campaigns.

"Governor, that sounds like a threat," she said.

"No, this is not a threat—this is a promise," he replied.

It was not surprising when she called his bluff and proceeded to send out a press release to her constituents to alert them about the threat the governor had delivered.

But she didn't stop there. She toured her district to address the issue directly with her constituents and went on air with local talk radio hosts who were active in galvanizing public opposition to the tax hike. She even put our phone number in the *Hendersonville Star News* with an invitation for people to call her at home.

"People were angry—they were very, very angry—that the governor would even think to do something like that," Diane told a reporter for the *Nashville Scene* in 1999. "And I'm new in politics. This may be the way politics are played all the time. This is my first experience ever in politics, and I don't like it."[7]

Colleagues in the legislature, even those within Diane's own party, admonished her for not "playing the game" the way it had always been played. She didn't care, however, if they thought her naive or idealistic—she saw through the arrogance and was convicted that the system had to change.[8]

Diane became one of the staunchest fighters against this unconstitutional income tax. After teaming up with then-State Senator Marsha Blackburn and then-State Representative Mae Beavers, Diane became known as one of the three "Killer Bs" in the statehouse. These three women—Black, Blackburn,

---

7   Liz Murray Garrigan, "Undaunted Diane," *Nashville Scene*, November 11, 1999.
8   Ibid.

and Beavers—were recognized as the elected officials most adamantly and publicly opposed to the proposed income tax. Not only did these fearless legislators stand up to the governor, but they rallied citizens to call their representatives and to protest in the streets, waving flags, carrying tea bags, or honking the horns of their cars and trucks as they drove past the Capitol.[9]

"That was what I considered the Tea Party before the Tea Party became vogue," Diane said, in a 2011 interview with *The Weekly Standard*. "Folks said, 'What do you think about us coming down and honking our horns?' I said, 'I love it! Come down! Let the elected officials know what you're thinking.'"[10]

Though her constituents fully supported Diane's actions, her opponents took measures to intimidate her.

"During that era when Diane stood up to Governor Sundquist, she felt threatened," said Barb. "On our walks through the neighborhood, she told me she was always looking over her shoulder. She had taken to running in the morning, but she felt afraid, which was unusual because she isn't usually fearful. I don't know that people really understood what she went through when she put up that fight."

---

9 For a more comprehensive account of the fight against the Tennessee income tax, see Phil Valentine, *Tax Revolt: The Rebellion Against an Overbearing, Bloated, Arrogant, and Abusive Government* (Nashville: Thomas Nelson, 2005).

10 Michael Warren, "Another Killer B in the House," *The Weekly Standard*, January 31, 2011.

Despite any uneasiness, Diane and her colleagues didn't regret a moment they had spent preventing the governor's desired income tax.

"We avoided what could have been a disastrous addition of a state income tax. Diane Black was one of the key figures in that fight," said former Lt. Gov. Ron Ramsey, who was a state senator at the time and one of the leaders of his chamber in the fight against the added tax. "We proved that we didn't need to raise taxes; we needed instead to live within our means and promote growth, which had the added effect of increasing revenues in other ways. A sales tax is fairer—everyone has to pay it and more than a quarter of our state revenues come from visitors to the state. Avoiding income tax keeps our government smaller and more manageable—less bloated."[11]

Diane, of course, agreed: "There were a lot of arguments that the state of Tennessee just couldn't make it without having this income tax. But if you look at Tennessee to see how we recovered [in 2002] as compared to some of these other states that were so heavily taxed, you'll see that we were able to come out of that economic downturn a whole lot sooner and better than those states."[12]

The threats and intimidation by Gov. Sundquist were an experience that immediately shaped Diane as an elected official. The traditional political practices she encountered

---

11 Interview with Ron Ramsey, October 2017.
12 Michael Warren, "Another Killer B in the House," The Weekly Standard, January 31, 2011.

were not only unsavory but they also convinced her that
effective leadership could succeed through transparency
and voicing the truth. The Sundquist "old boy politics" of
misleading the public and misinterpreting the Tennessee
constitution could be successively defeated by standing her
ground, resisting with determination, and speaking directly
to the voters. These were lessons that proved invaluable
throughout her political career.

The road to reforming TennCare would be long and
arduous. Many important changes wouldn't happen until Phil
Bredesen was elected governor and Diane had moved on to
the state Senate, but blocking Gov. Sundquist's income tax two
years in a row was a strong start toward fiscal sanity. It was
a great moment of citizens and elected officials refusing to be
bullied by the governor, Senate Speaker Pro Tem Bob Rochelle,
or Speaker of the House Jimmy Naifeh. It was also a great
example of the power of elected representatives standing for
principle and providing leadership at a critical moment.

Challenging the Speaker

Most brand-new representatives spend their first year in
the legislature learning the ropes, not necessarily challenging
the governor, especially one from their own party. But even as
a freshman, Diane demonstrated her unstoppable spirit. And
she was only getting started. On two separate occasions, she
also went toe-to-toe with the Speaker of the House, Jimmy
Naifeh.

When Diane joined the General Assembly, the Tennessee House was still controlled by the Democrats—they held a 54-45 majority—and the Republicans had a longstanding tradition of capitulating to Democrat party leadership. This was most evident in the minority party's support of Democrat Jimmy Naifeh, who had been a state representative since 1974 and Speaker of the House since 1991. The Speaker presides over legislative sessions in the House, assigns representatives to various committees, and appoints the committee chairmen. Naifeh was known for rewarding supporters with coveted leadership positions or desired committee assignments, which gave moderate Republicans an incentive to continue voting for him.

When Diane was first elected, Naifeh was resistant to setting her up with an office or assigning a designated parking spot—the Democrats expected Charles Robert Bone to win the seat, and they weren't enthused about rolling out the welcome mat for another Republican. During her first organizational session in January of 1999, Diane watched in disbelief as Naifeh was reelected as Speaker with full support of the Republicans. She started asking her colleagues why everyone just fell in line, rather than opposing his election.

After a few more election cycles, Diane decided it was time that someone in her party step up. At the start of the 2003 legislative session, Republican minority leader Tre Hargett turned down the nomination for Speaker. When no other Republicans were audacious enough to run against

Naifeh, Rep. Tre Hargett nominated Diane as an opposition candidate, and Rep. Bill Dunn seconded the motion.

"If you ever want to be in leadership, you have to act like you're leading," she told her colleagues. "We have to have a candidate to run against Jimmy Naifeh." Other colleagues then called her and asked her to do it. What was funny was how voting by order of the alphabet gave the incumbent Speaker a bit of a scare. Out of the first ten votes, six of them went to Diane. Naifeh looked worried for a few seconds. Obviously she lost, but she was bold enough to challenge him and make a point to her own party. And eleven of her colleagues supported Naifeh even though they had their own candidate as a nominee.

Diane knew it wasn't likely she would win that election—but she considered herself a fighter with the courage to demonstrate that if you want to gain leadership you have to act like a leader.

Ron Ramsey was famous for saying, "It matters who governs." But you have to act like you're leading in order to govern, even if you're in the minority. That's what Diane was trying to get across to the other legislators in her party. It took a lot of gumption—none of those men in her group would do it because they feared losing the committee assignments or chairmanships they wanted.

After that incident, the Republicans changed their bylaws to state that the party leader would automatically be the candidate for Speaker.[13] The "Naifeh Eleven," as his

---

13 "House's 'Naifeh 11' out of working order," *The City Paper*, December 13, 2004.

Republican supporters came to be called, were precluded from caucus leadership and lost their party's support in the following primary. This became an important moment in the Republicans' eventually gaining the majority in the House.

The other way that Diane challenged Speaker Naifeh was in her push to ban smoking in the Legislative Plaza. Given that Tennessee has long ranked among the top five tobacco-growing states in the country, the state also has had lower taxes on tobacco and fewer restrictions on smoking,[14] and many anti-smoking bills ended up killed in the House Agricultural Committee, which was headed by a tobacco farmer.[15] But despite tobacco's prominence in the Tennessee economy, public health concerns about the effects of tobacco use were only growing stronger.

Diane began bringing up the issue of smoking in the Legislative Plaza, but her proposed bills continually ended up killed by the committees to which Naifeh delegated them. It didn't help any that not only was Naifeh not fond of Diane, but his family had been in the grocery wholesale business, supplying merchandise like cigarettes to convenience stores.[16] But she was determined—she persisted in presenting her bill to ban smoking in the Legislative Plaza.

Finally, Naifeh told her, "Well, any bill can come to the floor if you can get two-thirds of the members to bring it to a vote."

14 Amanda Fallin and Stanton A. Glantz, "Tobacco-Control Policies in Tobacco-Growing States: Where Tobacco Was King," *The Milbank Quarterly*, Volume 93, Issue 2, June 2015, 319–358.
15 William Hinton, "The King Is Dead," *Nashville Scene*, August 3, 2006.
16 *Ibid.*

Diane rallied support from not only her own party members but also Democrats who wanted to see the smoking cease in the Plaza—including then-State Senator Rosalind Kurita who, like Diane, was a registered nurse and had an affinity for public health issues. Both women also counted tobacco farmers among their constituents, but the farmers weren't necessarily opposed to their efforts. Though tobacco crops made up all or part of their livelihood, the farmers understood the health risks and didn't want their own children smoking.

Naifeh, knowing Diane had the support to bring the issue to a vote, brought her into his office to negotiate changes to the existing rules. The end result was that smoking was only allowed in carpeted areas and prohibited on the linoleum— which is where legislators voted. When Naifeh asked her how she planned to enforce the new law, Diane responded by going out and buying toy squirt guns. She gave these water pistols to the sergeant at arms and told him to squirt anyone caught smoking in the wrong area. She also doled out candy cigarettes to all the smokers to enjoy while the legislature was in session.

Diane told Speaker Naifeh that if her bill passed, she would smoke a cigar with him in the Speaker's box, which she did.

As a nurse, Diane naturally was concerned that legislators still smoked on the House and Senate floors. In 2003, the state government spent $1.2 million to clean the walls and ceiling of the Capitol and remove the soot and nicotine that had accumulated over decades of smoking inside the building.

Even more importantly, schoolchildren regularly toured the statehouse and sat in the galleries to watch legislators in action—which meant that while representatives discussed public policy, they were also puffing away, sending out secondhand smoke throughout the room and sending the wrong message to those young spectators.

Diane and Sen. Kurita spent about eight years advocating for antismoking legislation, much of which was only finally implemented after she was elected to the state Senate. Over those years, public buildings increasingly became smoke-free. On June 20, 2006, Gov. Phil Bredesen, who had taken office in 2003, signed a bill that officially prohibited smoking in all government-owned buildings, and a year later the Non-Smoker Protection Act, banning smoking in all enclosed public places and workplaces in the state, was signed into law.

The fight for life

While serving in the House, Diane began several initiatives to improve health care for Tennesseans, especially the elderly, but the most important political issue for her has always been the life of the unborn.

Years ago, Tennessee had in place a number of commonsense statutes on abortion, such as informed consent, a forty-eight-hour wait time between the consultation and the procedure, and hospitalization for abortions performed after the first trimester. In 1992, however, Planned Parenthood and the ACLU filed a suit against the state to challenge these restrictions, claiming they placed an undue burden on women. The Davidson County trial court struck down certain provisions as unconstitutional while upholding other statutes that the justices themselves modified. Eight years and many appeals later, the case made its way to the Tennessee Supreme Court.

On September 15, 2000, ruling on *Planned Parenthood v. Sundquist*, the state Supreme Court affirmed the decision to strike down the General Assembly's abortion restrictions, declaring that the Tennessee Constitution provided greater protections for abortion rights than the US Constitution did. The court also declared that any abortion regulations would also have to pass strict scrutiny—the highest level of judicial review.

Conservative legislators and pro-life advocates across the state were appalled by this decision. How was it possible that a state so firmly founded on life and faith could have a constitution that allotted greater abortion freedoms than the federal government? It was simply unconscionable. The resulting lack of regulations for abortion procedures resulted in Tennessee's becoming the state with the third-highest percentage of out-of-state abortions. Because of the Supreme Court ruling, Tennessee became an abortion destination.

Following the ruling, the Tennessee GOP and right-to-life organizations got straight to work. The principal strategy was to craft and pass an amendment to the state constitution to return the regulatory power over abortion to the people through their elected representatives in the General Assembly.

When the Tennessee legislature enacts a new statute, identical bills are presented in both the House and the Senate. In the Senate, the bill goes straight to the floor for a vote, but in the House it starts in a subcommittee or a committee, which has to pass it by a simple majority before the bill goes for a vote on the House floor. If the bill passes both chambers, it's then sent to the governor for signature.

In the case of a constitutional amendment, the legislation takes the form of a joint resolution between the House and the Senate. Joint resolutions can begin in either the House or Senate, and they generally move through the chamber of the sponsoring member first. The joint resolution has to pass two consecutive assemblies—by a majority vote in both chambers during the first assembly and by a two-thirds majority during the second. The resolution is then added to the ballot for the next gubernatorial election to be decided upon by voters. That means a constitutional amendment can be put to a referendum only every four years.

In light of these procedures, changing the Tennessee Constitution also meant recruiting and electing many more pro-life legislators to the House and Senate to secure the majority necessary to pass the amendment and put it to a public vote.

The initial legislation was Senate Joint Resolution 110, sponsored by State Senator David Fowler, which presented a provision that stated, "Any right to an abortion in Tennessee shall only be such as is protected under the United States

Constitution as interpreted by the United States Supreme Court, from time to time. Nothing in this Constitution shall be interpreted to require that any state funds be appropriated by the state to fund or pay for any abortion."

The third and final vote on SJR 110 took place in May 2001, and the resolution moved over to the House where a different state representative sponsored it. But action on the resolution was repeatedly deferred by a Health and Human Resources subcommittee until the resolution finally died in 2002.

The legislation that took its place was Senate Joint Resolution 127, originally filed in 2003 by Sen. Fowler, which became the ballot initiative known as Amendment 1 to be voted on in the governor's election of 2014. After SJR 127 passed the Tennessee Senate in 2004, the resolution moved over to the House where Diane sponsored and lobbied for passage.

SJR 127 stated, "Nothing in this Constitution secures or protects a right to abortion or requires the funding of an abortion. The people retain the right through their elected state representatives and state senators to enact, amend, or repeal statutes regarding abortion, including, but not limited to, circumstances of pregnancy resulting from rape or incest or when necessary to save the life of the mother."

The legislation crafted in response to *Planned Parenthood v. Sundquist* was deeply personal for Diane. As an ER nurse, she has seen life and death as close as anyone will ever see it, and she has seen it over and over again. She is a passionate defender of the rights of unborn children, and she is a woman of deep faith, compassion, and generosity.

Although abortion is fundamentally a moral issue and a faith issue regarding life, Diane traces her particular feelings about abortion providers back to an incident in 1990 when she was working as an emergency room nurse at Hendersonville Hospital. A young woman about twenty-two years old entered the waiting room after undergoing an incomplete abortion at a nearby clinic that wasn't properly regulated. Following the complications, the woman hadn't been able to reach anyone at the clinic's after-hours phone number, and she had waited at home bleeding for hours before seeking emergency medical care. But by the time she'd reached the emergency room, there was nothing they could do to save her, and the young woman died that evening.

Diane was convinced that young woman's life could have been spared if proper regulations had been in place to protect her well-being—protections that were in place before the court ruling and that needed to be reinstated.

In the ensuing years, SJR 127 would fail seven years in a row—despite passing in the Senate each time and having strong support in the House—because Speaker Naifeh kept sending it to a House committee he knew would kill it. The resolution was revived, however, during each subsequent legislative session.

Naifeh was known to send Diane's bills to committees that would keep her legislation from public comment or an actual vote on the floor, but when it came to this constitutional amendment, she wasn't going to back down. Once again, she made a bold and risky move to defy Speaker Naifeh's obstruction, one that truly demonstrates her unstoppable determination on matters of utmost importance.

Diane knew that there were legislators who professed a pro-life stance to their constituents but voted differently when they were in Nashville. She also knew there was a little-known rule in the House that she could exploit in order call her legislation out of committee and onto the floor for a vote as she had done for her antismoking legislation. This maneuver would serve two purposes: Naifeh's administrative obstruction on SJR 127 would be overridden, and those purported pro-life representatives would have to go on record one way or another.

Diane invoked House Rule 53, which allowed a bill that had been in committee for seven days to be recalled by two-thirds of the state representatives and placed on the calendar.[17] She had duly submitted notice of her motion with the chief clerk a few days in advance, and her intent was to secure a vote to recall the resolution out of committee so that it could be put to an official vote. Early in the session, Speaker Naifeh acknowledged that the representatives were faced with a special order, and he recommended that this special order be brought ahead of the forty-four other bills they were due to discuss that day. After

---

17 See Temporary House Rules of Order, from the 106th General
   Assembly, http://www.capitol.tn.gov/House/rules.html, last retrieved
   December 30, 2017.

Chief Clerk Burney Durham read Diane's request, she stood up to speak.

On Monday, May 10, 2004, Joi Wasill was among Diane's supporters in the gallery when she made her bold move. Joi is the founder and executive director of Decisions, Choices, and Options, a nonprofit educational organization in Hendersonville, and she has worked with Diane on pro-life causes in Sumner County for many years.

"We were all in the gallery when Diane stood up," said Joi. "I can still see her in a red suit, pushing her chair back and standing up. It all seemed to move in slow motion. Then she spoke into the microphone and the room went dead quiet. It was as still as a monastery. No one said a word."[18]

"Mr. Speaker, I'm moved to recall SJR 127 from the Public Health subcommittee as provided for in House Rule Number 53," said Diane.

Speaker Naifeh acknowledged her motion and that it had been properly seconded.

"Members of the House, SJR 127 has fifty-four cosponsors and it deserves an opportunity for full consideration and debate in this chamber," Diane began. "Five members of a subcommittee should not have the ability to hold a bill, or in this case a resolution, in committee when there are a majority of members in favor of this resolution and have signed on as cosponsors."

18 Interview with Joi Wasill, October 2017.

Diane knew that her fight that day was not so much about the content of SJR 127 but about the committee system that had been part of the General Assembly's regular order for two hundred years. She went on to remind her colleagues that they suspended the rules on a daily basis—including when they debated the lottery and when they considered the resolution to limit smoking in the Capitol.

"I do have respect for the committee system, and I don't suggest that we would take Rule 53 lightly. However, this is a different matter. This is a matter of life and this should be given every consideration, especially since there are fifty-four sponsors," she said.

Diane reminded the House that Tennessee once had commonsense protections for women and the unborn that were overturned by the Supreme Court ruling. Getting SJR 127 out of committee and onto the floor for a vote was an increasingly urgent matter.

Rep. Kim McMillan, a Democrat, stood up to vehemently oppose Diane's motion on the basis that the legislative committee system was being usurped by political machinations. A more passionate plea for doing business by committee has perhaps never been uttered.

"Let me be very, very clear," said Rep. McMillan. "This is not a vote on the merits of any particular piece of legislation, and anyone who categorizes that as such is not telling you the truth. The truth is that this motion is asking you to deconstruct the fabric of our system and that which makes us a functional legislative body."

Diane was not alone in her effort—Rep. Bill Dunn seconded her motion and spoke up in defense of the motion.

"How can using a rule be breaking the rules?" Rep. Dunn asked. "We wouldn't have this rule unless it was meant to be used. And if today is not a day to use number 53, then I don't know when is . . . today is a day that will test each one of us as individuals as to what kind of people we are."

In her closing remarks, Diane said, "I want to remind this body that this was not an easy thing for me to do. I know that there has been talk that this was a political move on my part. I want to assure each one of you in this General Assembly that it was not a political move. This is something I believe in from my head to the bottom of my toes . . . The dangers of removing these commonsense protections are what bring me here today because I want to protect every woman. That is the reason I'm in this well."[19]

Diane's hope that day was to secure sixty-six ayes on her motion to get SJR 127 on the calendar for a vote, and then to pass SJR 127 in time for it to be added to the ballot for the 2006 gubernatorial election. But after her motion failed 52-36, with three members not voting, it would take another ten years for the referendum to finally be put on a ballot.

---

19 For a complete audio of the proceedings, see Tennessee General Assembly, House Session, May 10, 2004, 4:04 p.m., Tape No. H-76.

"Diane is one of the bravest, most gifted people I know," said Joi. "She wasn't afraid to challenge this powerful man for a cause she believed in with all her heart."

There are few issues as important to Diane than fighting for the unborn. She wasn't about to stand down when Speaker Naifeh kept sending her bills to be killed in committee, and her fight to change the Tennessee Constitution was only heating up.

Chapter 6

A New Majority

The 2000 Tennessee Supreme Court decision galvanized state Republicans and provided a key issue on which to challenge Democrat senators and representatives as they came up for reelection in ensuing years. In a state that had been largely blue since Reconstruction, building a conservative Republican majority often seemed like a very steep hill to climb, but with the constitutional amendment now at stake, the caucus had an even stronger imperative.

By 2004, Diane had served three two-year terms in the Tennessee House of Representatives, and her gumption and effectiveness had not gone unnoticed. Ron Ramsey began urging her to run for a seat in the upper chamber. It was a risky move—she would be giving up a safe seat in the House to run against Democrat Jo Ann Graves, the Senate Speaker pro Tempore, who represented the 18th Senate District, which then included Robertson County and almost all of Sumner County.

Certain House Republicans didn't want her to run for Senate. They wanted *someone* to run against Jo Ann Graves but not Diane—she was effective in the House, and they didn't think Graves could be beat.

"The leaders of the House Republican Caucus didn't want Diane to leave because they felt that they were on the cusp of taking over," noted Lance Frizzell, who was press secretary for the Republican House Caucus at the time. "Diane was one of the few representatives with strong leadership skills—her colleagues thought she could be Speaker in a few years. But Ron knew that Diane was the only one who could defeat Graves. He said you had to have someone like Diane—someone who was willing to run against the Speaker on principle."[20]

Diane met with Ron Ramsey and Bob Davis, who was the chairman of the Tennessee Republican Party at the time, at the party headquarters in Nashville to discuss the opportunity.

"We want you to run for state Senate," Ron told her.

"I don't know, I'm pretty happy in the House," Diane replied. "I have a good career path here."

"No, we need you in the Senate. You can win."

"So you've done some polling?" she asked.

When Ron and Bob admitted they hadn't, she told them to survey Graves's district and get back to her.

As it turned out, the polls didn't look good for Diane. The incumbent had good approval ratings in her district and a strong probability of reelection.

20 Interview with Lance Frizzell, October 2017.

A couple of weeks later, Diane returned to the Tennessee GOP headquarters for a follow-up meeting.

"Did the polling come back?"

"Yeah, the polling's back," Ron said.

"Well, how was it?"

Ron and Bob didn't dare let her see it. Instead, they just said, "Not bad."

"So I can win?"

Over the years, Ron has enjoyed telling the story about how he said yes, while secretly crossing his fingers. He didn't reveal to her how unlikely a win it would be until after the results of the election.[21] What no one wanted was for Diane to run against an incumbent state senator and end up shut out of the entire legislature if she lost, but it was a gamble they were willing to take.

Diane's campaign for the state Senate was an exciting race. The issue of abortion laws motivated her and her base to get her elected. Tennessee Right to Life and other advocates campaigned on her behalf, pointing out to district constituents that while Graves claimed to Sumner County conservatives that she stood with them on their pro-life principles, her voting record in Nashville proved otherwise. When SJR 110 or SJR 127 had come up for votes, Graves repeatedly voted to weaken or gut the bills, only voting in favor once all other efforts to weaken it or prevent its passing had failed.

---

21 Interview with Ron Ramsey, October 2017.

While pro-lifers were actively campaigning for Diane, Graves's campaign was attacking her and putting out mean-spirited ads accusing her of all sorts of things. They tried to portray her as someone who went down to Nashville and wasn't who she said she was, when it was Jo Ann who was doing exactly that. One of the most disgusting political ads was one that took Diane's face and twisted her appearance into a Halloween lantern that made her appear to be an evil character. This political piece was so offensive that I worked with Diane's campaign manager to release a personal note about who Diane truly was, which was mailed out to district constituents without Diane's knowledge.

The public attack ads were bad enough, but we also got personally harassed. People came onto our property; we had terrible voice mails left at the house. One of Diane's campaign managers was effectively run off from the campaign after receiving threatening calls—the person told her the color of her car and where it was parked. They said they knew where she was and they were going to "take care of her," or something equally intimidating.

But as I've said before, my wife is not so easily intimidated. When she has her mind set on something, she won't be deterred.

In the last two weeks before the election, Graves's campaign began to sense she was in trouble, despite having a significant lead in funding. As the race got closer, we were told that Phil Bredesen put another $50,000 or more into

Graves's campaign. The Tennessee GOP told us we needed to match this fresh influx of cash, but we refused. We insisted we would win or lose this election on our messaging alone— not by money.

I remember the excitement of election night, November 2, 2004, as early returns came in from outlying counties. Diane was losing these outlying precincts, but not by as big of a margin as she should have been. We knew from these early returns that she was going to win the Senate seat. We could sense we were going to win, but we had friends go to bed that night thinking she'd lost because all through the evening the television reports showed she was behind in the results.

As the night went on, things got a bit more interesting. When polls closed at 7:00 p.m., the early vote came in about ten minutes after the hour as expected from Sumner County. Jamie Clary, her campaign manager (now mayor of Hendersonville), called over to Robertson County for the early vote, but they said they couldn't release it yet.

Jamie called twenty minutes after seven, but again they said they couldn't release it. At 7:30 he called again, but to no avail.

"I'm concerned about this," Jamie said.

"I'm concerned too," I replied. "We should have had that vote by now."

We called Robertson County together at 7:40, but officials still wouldn't give us the results, so we alerted the state Republican Party who told Robertson County to produce the results immediately or they'd be there with a court order to obtain the results.

Although Diane lost Robertson County by only a small margin, the delay was troubling—even though our friends in Robertson County assured us no one would have done anything suspicious. I still have no idea why it took us until almost eight o'clock to get the results of the early vote, which was a delay that had not happened prior and has not happened since.

Though we felt it all along, Diane's victory wasn't official until about 11:00 p.m., when we were at 100 percent of precincts reporting. The election outcome surprised many political pundits and even those who had supported her. There were quite a few people who had thought she could win, but there were also quite a good number who did not think it was possible to win against Graves with the governor's support.

After Diane won her seat in the Senate, Ron Ramsey and Bob Davis showed her the results of their initial district polling.

"I'm not sure I would have run if I'd seen that poll," she said.

"Exactly! That's why we didn't let you see it," replied Ron.

Sixteen of the thirty-three state senators were up for reelection that year, and eleven of them were Democrats, who controlled the Senate 18-15. When Bedford County's Jim Tracy and Diane won their two seats in 2004, the Senate had its first Republican majority since the Reconstruction era that followed the Civil War. It would take two more years to gain a majority in the House.

Despite the new 17-16 Republican majority, when the legislature convened its next organizational session, state senators reelected their longstanding Speaker, John Wilder, a Democrat who had held the post since 1971. Like Naifeh, Wilder had often rewarded bipartisan support with appointments to committee chairs, but after the elections in November of 2006, Republicans were pressured to adhere to party discipline and support their candidate for lieutenant governor.

As a result, on January 9, 2007, Ron Ramsey was elected Speaker of the Senate and lieutenant governor by the unanimous vote of Republicans and one Democrat, Rosalind Kurita—the same senator who had partnered with Diane to combat indoor smoking. Ron became the first Republican to serve as Speaker of the Senate in 140 years. Ramsey went on to be the longest-serving Republican Speaker in state history.

During her time in the state Senate, Diane served as the assistant floor leader of the Senate Republican Caucus. She was a member of the Senate Government Operations Committee and the Senate Finance, Ways and Means Committee, which gave her essential experience with tax issues and crafting budgets. She held leadership posts including vice chairman of the General Welfare, Health and Human Resources Committee.

In 2006, Diane was elected chairman of the Tennessee Senate Republican Caucus—the first woman to hold the position in the history of the state. As chairman, she presided over caucus meetings, directed fundraising efforts, and helped other Republican candidates get elected.

Enacting policies that matter

While in the Tennessee General Assembly, Diane focused on a number of standard-setting policies and causes that improved the safety, well-being, and prosperity of people in Tennessee. She was known as a champion for children and seniors, traditional family values, fiscal responsibility, and supporting small-business owners. Given her long career as a nurse, health care was especially Diane's strength and focus.

In 2003, Democrat Phil Bredesen succeeded Don Sundquist as governor. He had campaigned on a promise to fix TennCare, pointing to his experience as a health-care executive. In February of 2004, Gov. Bredesen addressed a joint convention of the House and Senate and made a series of proposals to restructure TennCare and incrementally reduce benefits until it was a more financially manageable program. His proposed changes included tailoring the benefit packages more specifically to various groups in the plan; reducing the number of prescriptions, hospital days, outpatient visits, physician visits, labs and X-rays that are covered every year; insisting on generic or over-the-counter drugs when available; a better system of cost sharing with enrollees; and a disease management program to bring better health to those with preventable illnesses and medical conditions.[22]

---

22 Phil Bredesen, "State of TennCare Address," Tennessee General Assembly in Joint Convention, Tuesday, February, 17, 2004, http://www.capitol.tn.gov/House/Archives/103GA/Publications/web%20journ%202004/02172004jc54.pdf.

Negotiations and legal battles over the proposed changes ensued for the next year or so, and by 2005, Bredesen was proposing to cut 323,000 TennCare enrollees from the roster.

Like most Republicans, Diane wanted to enact significant reforms to cut TennCare costs, but as a health-care professional, she wanted it done in a way that was both smart and compassionate. When the governor initially proposed removing 323,000 people from TennCare, Diane, Ron Ramsey, and Senator Jim Bryson worked with Finance Commissioner Dave Goetz to find funds to alleviate the pain that would be caused by such a broad and unfocused approach. Their suggestions were, however, rejected. Rep. Joey Hensley, a Republican and a TennCare doctor, had also proposed a way to keep from cutting 67,000 TennCare recipients, but his suggestions were also rebuffed.[23]

Ultimately, 200,000 enrollees were unceremoniously dropped from TennCare and another 400,000 had their prescription benefits reduced to five a month. Many of those affected were the working poor—often people who were suffering from a preexisting condition that kept them from securing private insurance but who made too much money to qualify for Medicaid.

The three senators were also among the thirty-four lawmakers from both the House and the Senate who asked Gov. Bredesen for a special session to address the fallout and suffering caused by the massive and indiscriminate

---

23 "GOP has a chance to show mettle on TennCare," *The Tennessean*, July 7, 2005.

cuts he had made. All of these lawmakers agreed that the TennCare program needed to be better managed, but there was also a human element at play that couldn't simply be disregarded.

Though Gov. Bredesen had succeeded in reducing TennCare to a program the state could afford, Diane was upset with the manner in which it unfolded and the interruption to many patients' essential medical care. Cancer patients arrived at the legislative offices to plead with their representatives. Others arrived with their catheters still inserted to gain sympathy. Whereas some wanted drastic reductions for the sake of the bottom line, Diane was more concerned with a soft glide and reduction of costs with minimal hardship— ensuring that both the budget and people's lives were kept in perspective and in balance.

Long-term health care

Though TennCare initially inspired Diane to run for public office, other health-care policies kept her busy while she was in the state legislature, such as passing a bill that provided more options for long-term health care for seniors.

When we lived in Maryland, Diane had worked for several years in home health care, so she understood the challenges and nuances of caring for the elderly and the disabled. In Tennessee, she discovered that the state was very far behind in long-term care policies and practices. TennCare spent 98 percent of its long-term care funding on institutional care, when home- and community-based options not only cost less but also improved patients' quality of life.

"Tennessee has been last in the nation for too long in the number of health-care choices for elderly and disabled citizens on Medicaid, a problem that has kept them from being able to stay in their homes and age with dignity," Diane said. "I know from speaking with citizens in my district that this is an issue that concerns many of them, and I can sympathize with their lack of options."[24]

For seven years, beginning when she was chairing the House Republican Health Care Task Force, Diane worked on an initiative to make home health care more accessible for Tennessee seniors. After entering the Senate, she continued her efforts while serving on the Senate General Welfare, Health, and Human Resources Committee and as a member of the legislature's Select Committee on Long-Term Care. The result was the Long-Term Care Community Choices Act of 2008, a program for self-directed care.

The legislation provided long-term care consumers who qualify for Medicaid with a monthly allowance that they can use to choose their particular services and providers, whether that's an in-home assistant, home modifications for disabilities, or other necessary expenses, with budget counseling and other accountability measures in place.

---

24 Tennessee Senate Republicans, "General Assembly passes budget and several key bills before adjourning 2008 legislative session," May 19, 2008, http://www.tngopsenate.com/general-assembly-passes-budget-and-several-key-bills-before-adjourning-2008-legislative-session.

"The legislation signed into law sets forward our guiding principles of what a long-term care system in Tennessee should look like," Diane said. "It moves toward a continuum of care that is seamless as the needs of the individual changes. In the end, this legislation should provide more choices for our seniors and disabled to help them 'age in place' in their homes."

The result of the legislation was more efficient coordination of care, improved access to care, expanded options in home and community-based services, and greater satisfaction among users. In 2008, Tennessee Association of Homes and Services for the Aging honored Diane with their Executive Leadership Award.

Protecting children of all ages

From the unborn to the very old, Diane is passionate about defending and caring for the most vulnerable populations. Despite our state's growing prosperity, she has discovered that not everyone in Tennessee is thriving as well as they should.

While she was in the state Senate, Diane discovered that Memphis had third-world mortality rates for newborn children. In response, she sponsored legislation that pairs nurses with at-risk families. The Nurse Family Partnership provides regular, in-home visiting nurse services to low-income, first-time mothers during pregnancy through the child's second birthday. The nurses educate mothers on proper nutrition and the importance of avoiding drugs and alcohol, and they show these moms how to provide standard care for their children.

The program works out of Memphis hospitals and has been quite successful in reducing the infant mortality rate in Shelby County.

Another group of children that Diane took to heart are those who have been bullied in school. Caitlin Nolan, a fifteen-year-old freshman from Oak Ridge, lobbied the Tennessee legislature to draft anti-bullying legislation after the same bully targeted her repeatedly for two years in middle school. When the bullying began to affect her grades and emotional health, Caitlin decided to fight for new rules to protect students.

"Any time a child is scared of school, when they're scared to learn, it's not just kids being kids," Caitlin told ABC News. "It's harassment. It wouldn't be allowed to happen in the real world, yet we're allowing it to happen in our schools."[25]

Despite the fact that Caitlin lived outside of Diane's district, Diane embraced Caitlin's cause and sponsored Senate Bill 1621, which Caitlin helped draft. The bill, which passed unanimously, prohibits bullying in every school district across Tennessee and sets guidelines for schools to establish proper prevention initiatives, reporting and investigation procedures, and appropriate remedial action.

After it was signed into law on May 2, 2005, the bill served as model legislation for other states seeking to encourage

---

25 Elizabeth Vargas, "Person of the Week: Caitlin Nolan," *ABC News*, April 29, 2005.

a safe and civil environment for students by discouraging harassment, intimidation, and bullying in their schools.

As it turned out, while I was at Aegis, our company president's daughter was being bullied at her school, and the procedures outlined in the anti-bullying bill were used to protect her. Although we had heard from others, it was heartening to hear directly from a friend and colleague that his daughter was protected by the very legislation that Diane had sponsored and passed into law.

About four years after the initial anti-bullying bill was passed, Diane introduced a follow-up measure to strengthen the legislation's provisions. Her 2009 SB 283 bill required local schools to include thirteen standards in their bullying policies, which ensured that the policies were more consistent across all Tennessee school systems.

"Bullying is a widespread problem among students nationwide," Diane said in a statement about the revised statute. "Research indicates that approximately 160,000 students avoid school every day for fear of being bullied."[26]

Some students who are bullied go on to commit suicide, though many other young people choose to kill themselves for reasons their parents may never understand. Hendersonville resident Clark Flatt is one such parent. His sixteen-year-

---

26 Tennessee Senate Republicans, "Legislation protecting children from child sexual predators advances in Senate," February 26, 2009, http://www.tngopsenate.com/legislation-protecting-children-from-child-sexual-predators-advances-in-senate.

old son Jason committed suicide one July day in 1992 after
a breakup with his girlfriend. Clark turned his grief into
a mission and started the Jason Foundation to promote
awareness of the "silent epidemic" of youth suicide.

After getting to know Clark, Diane became the lead
sponsor on the Jason Flatt Act of 2007, which requires at least
two hours of suicide prevention training for all Tennessee
teachers and principals each school year, using a curriculum
of their choosing that instructs on recognizing the signs and
symptoms of troubled youth and those who may be at risk
for suicide.

She also worked on a number of bills in the state
Senate to better protect children from sex offenders. While
a member of the Senate Judiciary Committee, she sponsored
a bill requiring law enforcement agencies to enter data into
the National Crime Information Center (NCIC) within two
hours of receiving a missing-child report. This rule brought
Tennessee into compliance with the federal Adam Walsh Act.

Signed into federal law in 2006, the Adam Walsh Child
Protection and Safety Act was one of a series of laws enacted
since 1994 that required states to maintain sex offender
registries, but its provisions required a certain baseline
standard for the registries, including required personal and
criminal information about offenders and tougher criminal
penalties for failing to register. States' failure to comply with
the Adam Walsh Act would result in an annual 10 percent
reduction in federal grants for fighting crime.

"This legislation makes sure that we are acting quickly to enter the needed information to alert law enforcement of a missing child," Diane said. "Hopefully, this will help us to bring these children safely home quicker."[27]

The law was named after the six-year-old son of John Walsh, host of *America's Most Wanted.* Adam was murdered by serial killer Ottis Toole in 1981.

In 2010, the Senate approved another bill Diane sponsored jointly with Rep. Debra Maggart that required the Board of Medical Examiners to deny or revoke the medical license of any doctor who is registered as a sex offender. The bill was first inspired by a local mother who took her eight-year-old daughter to see their family doctor. The mom had an uneasy feeling about the man, which prompted her to look up the physician in the Tennessee Bureau of Investigation sex offender database. He had been charged with first-degree rape, sodomy, and sexual abuse after a six-year "relationship" with his teen stepdaughter, but he pled down his charges to misdemeanor sexual conduct.

Two other states had already denied the doctor a medical license, but nothing in Tennessee law prevented him from practicing family medicine in our state until Diane and Debra's legislation.

"Sex offenders should not have direct contact with patients in the practice of medicine," said Diane. "This legislation

27 *Ibid.*

gives the Board direction to make sure this does not happen in Tennessee."[28]

The two lawmakers worked together on similar legislation, including a 2009 statute that permitted recorded interviews of an abused child by a forensic interviewer at a child advocacy center to be admissible in court. Allowing a videotaped interview to be used in place of live testimony protects young victims from the secondary traumatization of facing their abuser in court and undergoing the oftentimes insensitive scrutiny of the defense.

The Tennessee Chapter of Children's Advocacy Centers recognized the two lawmakers for their commitment to preventing and punishing severe child abuse—in late 2009 Diane and Debra were presented with the association's Child Protection Investigative Team Leadership Award.

"This award is very special to me," said Diane. "I am humbled to receive recognition from those who are on the front lines of protecting children in Tennessee. We look forward to continuing to work with child advocates in our efforts to help these children who have suffered severe physical and emotional trauma."[29]

The bill was challenged in 2012 when a judge in a child rape case ruled that video testimony was hearsay and thus

---

28 State of Tennessee State Senate, "Black's Legislation to ensure that physicians who are registered sex offenders are not granted medical license passes full Senate," March 25, 2010.

29 State of Tennessee General Assembly, "Sen. Black and Rep. Maggart honored by Child Protection Advocates for their work on behalf of abused children," November 23, 2009.

inadmissible as evidence, and that the state legislature had overstepped its bounds when determining what evidence the court could consider.[30] The Tennessee Supreme Court, however, later overruled the judge and concluded that the statute violated no constitutional standards.[31]

Yes on 1

Diane's fiercest fight was the one she had started in the House, carried into the Senate, and continued long after she was serving in the US Congress. Though SJR 127, the joint resolution to put a constitutional amendment on abortion to a public referendum, had failed year after year, once the Republican majority in the Tennessee legislature had reached a critical mass, Democrats and other opponents could no longer defeat the bill in committee or on the floor.

SJR 127 was finally approved by both the House and Senate in 2009, but the Constitutional amendment process required that it pass it two consecutive assemblies. In 2010, Diane was elected to Congress and passed down her legislation to a Senate colleague to ensure the resolution made it the rest of the way to the ballot. SJR 127 passed the Tennessee General Assembly again in 2011 with unanimous Republican support and the backing of several respected Democrats. The resolution could then be added to the ballot

---

30 Stefanie Ingersoll, "Man acquitted of child rape in landmark case," *The Leaf Chronicle*, August 28, 2015.

31 State of Tennessee v. Barry D. McCoy, No. M2013-00912-SC-R11-CD (2014), https://www.tncourts.gov/sites/default/files/mccoybarryopn.pdf.

during the next election for governor, which would occur on Tuesday, November 4, 2014.

Leading up to the referendum, Diane was actively involved in the Yes on 1 campaign to secure the votes for the amendment. The state Supreme Court decision had rendered Tennessee the most liberal state in the union on abortion. Yes on 1 was about restoring commonsense protections for the women who make this very difficult choice—it was a compassionate step to take and one that we believed in deeply.

The Yes on 1 campaign, which spent about $1.5 million in grassroots support of the amendment, was outspent by the No on 1 campaign by three to one, which received donations from the ACLU and from Planned Parenthood organizations as far away as California, Washington, Massachusetts, and Florida. The opposition's messaging painted the supporters of the amendment as radical and extreme. Far-left groups called the proposal the "Taliban amendment" and "the next battleground in the war on women."

Such extreme, untruthful rhetoric is such a great example of what Diane has continuously fought against. That abortion is associated with sex trafficking and hardcore pornography, which abuse and demean women, could be a war on women is one of the greatest battles she has consistently fought. As a nurse, a mother, and a grandmother, the idea that her actions would harm women is ludicrous but is the fodder of political propaganda.

Diane felt that the truth of the matter was being unfairly obscured. In an op-ed to *The Tennessean*, she explained,

"Amendment 1 will not ban abortion in our state. It will instead give all Tennesseans a say by empowering our elected representatives to enact protections for women and unborn children that were wrongly struck down by unelected justices at the state Supreme Court. This includes informed-consent laws so that women know of any health risks associated with their abortion—a requirement that already exists for most other major surgeries—and regular inspections of abortion facilities to ensure compliance with health regulations."[32]

A month before the 2014 elections, while Tennesseans were being bombarded by television advertisements from both sides, Diane and I discussed what more we should do to ensure that this long-fought-for amendment to protect unborn babies could be passed. We agreed to personally donate $500,000 to the Tennesseans for Yes on 1 political action committee, which paid for direct mail advertising to support the measure.

That November, Tennessee voters approved passage of Amendment 1 with a 53-47 percent margin. Although Diane and I were the biggest private funders of the Yes on 1 campaign, the faith community and other pro-life advocates must receive the greater credit for their on-the-ground efforts to ensure this campaign was ultimately successful. The constitutional amendment enabled Tennessee to establish legal regulations of clinics and abortions for the first time

---

32 Diane Black, "Yes on 1 the compassionate choice," *The Tennessean*, October 20, 2014.

in more than a decade—a huge victory to protect pregnant women and the unborn.

"It took until November 4, 2014, to secure a vote, and though Diane was already in Congress by that point, she had been instrumental in working toward our hard-won victory," noted Ron Ramsey. "She has been so influential in this area that, once in Congress, she inherited Mike Pence's pro-life legislation when he ran for governor of Indiana in 2012."[33]

No sooner had we won that victory than the method of counting votes was challenged in court. Three years later, the United States Court of Appeals for the Sixth Circuit ruled that the vote counting methods were, in fact, valid.

"Plaintiffs' arguments amount to little more than a complaint that the campaigns in support of Amendment 1, operating withing the framework established by state law, turned out to be more successful than the campaigns against Amendment 1," the ruling stated.[34]

The court's decision was certainly a welcome relief for all the citizens and legislators who fought for many years to enact the amendment to the Tennessee constitution.

---

33 Interview with Ron Ramsey, October 2017.

34 Anita Wadhwani, "Appeals court upholds vote count on Tennessee abortion measure Amendment 1," *The Tennessean*, January 9, 2018.

Chapter 7

US Congressman Black

In July of 2009, Democrats in the US House of Representatives, led by Speaker Nancy Pelosi, unveiled an extensive plan to overhaul the US health-care system. Less than a year later, on March 23, 2010, President Obama signed the resulting legislation, the Patient Protection and Affordable Care Act (ACA), into law, which is generally referred to as Obamacare.

From Diane's position in the Tennessee legislature, the health-care reform initiative in Congress felt a bit like déjà vu. She saw Obamacare as basically TennCare on steroids, and if TennCare had adversely impacted our state finances and health-care delivery, she dreaded what the consequences of the ACA would be for the nation.

Diane wasn't the only one worried about Obamacare. Voters across the country were frustrated by a still-sluggish economy and galvanized by the burgeoning Tea Party movement. In the midterm elections in November of 2010, Republicans gained sixty-three seats in the House to take the majority and six Senate seats to reduce the Democrats' previous supermajority.

That November, Diane was among those Republicans taking over the US House of Representatives—the first woman to represent Tennessee's 6th Congressional District, a seat previously held by President James K. Polk and Vice President Al Gore, among others.

Back in 2009, Diane had felt called to serve in Congress because she had helped reform TennCare in our state and thought she could have an impact on health-care policy in Washington. Bart Gordon, a moderate Democrat, was stepping down from his seat representing the 6th Congressional District, which was then comprised of seventeen counties north, south, and east of Nashville, along with parts of Cheatham and Van Buren counties. Though the 6th District had sent Gordon to Congress for thirteen consecutive terms, and Al Gore before him for four terms, its constituents had become increasingly conservative and Republican. Bart Gordon likely saw the writing on the wall, especially after voting for the ACA, and his retirement from Congress created an opportunity for Republican contenders.

The Republican primary on August 5, 2010, was a tight race. Facing off against businesswoman Lou Ann Zelenik and State Senator Jim Tracy, Diane won the primary with a slim margin—she had 31 percent of the vote, while Ms. Zelenik and Jim won about 30 percent each. In the general election, however, Diane won all of the counties in the district, defeating her Democrat opponent, Brett Carter, with 67 percent of the vote.

On January 5, 2011, Diane was sworn in as a freshman member of the 112th Congress. Our children and grandchildren, as well as numerous friends and supporters, went to DC to watch the ceremony. Only children were allowed onto the House floor, so Diane took our three grandsons, Warren, Joseph, and Dylan. Since there were only a few seats in the House gallery, I gathered with the rest of the family in a separate room within the Capitol to watch the events on a television.

As the House was gathering, Boehner walked up the aisle to the applause of his Republican colleagues and greeted people in the seats. Our grandson Warren, who was standing near the aisle, reached out his hand, and Boehner graciously stopped to shake hands with him. The following morning, a picture of the moment ended up on the front page of the *Wall Street Journal.*

Following the swearing-in ceremony, the first act was to vote for the Speaker. Now that the Republicans held the majority in the House, they elected John Boehner from Ohio, thereby unseating Nancy Pelosi. We watched Boehner arrive at the Speaker's podium where Pelosi stood holding the Speaker's gavel in her hands, ostensibly to hand it over to Boehner. But as she started speaking, she kept holding onto the gavel.

As Pelosi kept talking and talking, our eight-year-old grandson Joey, said to Diane, "She's never going to give up that hammer!"

Earlier that day, Diane had gone ahead of us to the Capitol, and I was walking around the National Mall with some of the family and grandchildren to keep the young boys busy. As we headed toward the Capitol, we passed the Air and Space Museum, and I soon realized we were walking on the very same sidewalk Diane and I had walked during our first date. The thought that God has a plan, and that life often comes full circle, stayed with me all day through the events. Who would have ever thought, when we had that first date that Sunday in 1978, that we would be a family walking the same sidewalk all these years later to see Diane sworn in to Congress?

Contending with political lies

In 1998, when Diane first ran for office, politics wasn't quite yet as vitriolic as things are today. Even though we had some unpleasantness in that first race for the Tennessee House of Representatives, it was nothing like the divisiveness we've seen since. And the 2010 race for the US House of Representatives was perhaps the most vicious campaign we have endured to date.

For the past seven years, some people on the far right have circulated a lie that Diane directed no-bid Tennessee state contracts to the drug testing company I founded, Aegis Sciences Corporation. A lot of time and money has been invested in circulating this untruth. The lie was originally created by the left—during Diane's 2008 reelection campaign for state Senate against attorney Jim Hawkins, the Tennessee

Democratic Party distributed a mailer that attacked her for the same unfounded allegation.

This lie was then given new life during Diane's 2010 congressional race. Lou Ann Zelenik's campaign produced a cartoonish television ad that depicted Diane handing an oversized check to a character meant to be me. The check for $1 million was payable to Aegis Sciences Corporation from Tennessee taxpayers and signed by Diane. A voiceover stated, "Black's spending spree included a million bucks for a drug testing company. The company's owner: Diane Black's husband. Diane Black—big spending that hurt every Tennessee family except hers."

The accusation in the ad suggests that Diane directed contracts to Aegis through insider dealing, but it's totally false. Aegis secured contracts two years before she was ever elected to office, and they were sealed competitive bids, not no-bid contracts. What's more, legislators don't vote on contracts; they vote on budgets that fund state government. The executive branch enters into contracts. And why would anyone think that, as a freshman legislator, Diane could have had any influence over anyone in state government? In addition, she was immediately in conflict with Governor Sundquist, the head of the executive branch of government, over the proposed state income tax. In fact, after Diane was elected to the legislature, Aegis lost—through a sealed, competitive bidding process— the largest state contract it had to a drug testing company from New Mexico. The assertion that Diane did, or even could, influence contracts is entirely fabricated.

Aegis legal counsel recommended, and I agreed, to ask Ms. Zelenik to take down the video and radio ads, but she wouldn't, so in July of 2010, the Aegis board of directors decided, again on counsel's recommendation, that Aegis sue her, her senate campaign, and her campaign manager for defamation and civil conspiracy. Ms. Zelenik has always portrayed this lawsuit as centering on Diane, but she wasn't involved. The Aegis board of directors, representing Aegis's many shareholders, decided on this complaint based on the recommendation of corporate legal counsel to protect the company's reputation. Diane is not an employee, officer, or shareholder in Aegis. She has her political world; I have my business world. Diane never wanted Aegis to enter into legal action in the first place because she rightly discerned that lawsuits have a habit of dragging on and on. And this one certainly has.

The trial court, and later the appellate court, found the attack ad's assertions to be "substantially true," because Diane, as a legislator, voted on the state budget. This decision baffles me. The only thing "substantially true" is that Aegis received $1 million from the State of Tennessee for services rendered. Nothing about the ad's *implications*, however, are true at all and are in fact defamatory for us both. Diane did not in any way "direct" this contract to us.

And yet this false allegation persists. No media sources have come to interview me as the founder and CEO of Aegis or ask if this story is true, nor have any reporters gone to the Tennessee state government to investigate the truth of the political advertisements. Bright Media, the agency that created the false and misleading spots, settled with Aegis out of court, agreeing to fund in perpetuity four summer camp scholarships to YMCA Camp Widjiwagan for children of Fred Bailey's Children Are People program. Jim Hawkins, Diane's opponent in 2008, has since admitted the lie was created by the Tennessee Democratic Party for his campaign and apologized to me personally for using the ad in his campaign for state Senate.

Political ads can be totally devoid of truth and paint someone as completely different from who they are. We don't run negative campaigns or do the things that have been done to us, which is why, when Diane's campaign team ran a television political ad in which she refuted these accusations, some of her supporters didn't like it—they'd never seen her do anything that came close to negative campaigning. But Diane will always fight back and overcome big obstacles, even egregious political lies.

In 2012 when Diane was up for reelection, we faced more lies from Ms. Zelenik's campaign, including the assertion that Diane voted to fund Obamacare, based on her votes on continuing resolutions in Congress, which are short-term funding measures that keep the government running.

"Diane Black voted to fund Obamacare, then she voted to repeal it. I guess she was for it before she was against it," said the narrator in the radio ad.

I have to laugh at the idea that anyone who has looked at Diane's record would believe such an assertion, even for a moment. Ms. Zelenik's campaign staff members have asserted that Diane should have voted against the continuing resolutions simply on principle, but they miss the bigger picture. Diane's record is clear: she voted twenty-six times in support of more than two dozen amendments and bills that would dismantle or entirely repeal the ACA or block mandatory funding.[35] [36] In fact, as a freshman congressman, Diane passed the first legislation to close a wasteful loophole within the ACA, which saved the taxpayers over $13 billion. Even President Obama agreed her sponsored legislation needed to be signed into law, which in essence repealed a portion of the ACA.

Regardless of the lies, Diane won the 2012 reelection with a two-to-one margin against Ms. Zelenik, her repeat opponent. Diane's constituents have been intelligent and informed enough to see for themselves that her voting record in Washington reflects their shared values.

The pro-life leader

Diane came to Congress already identified as a staunch and fearless champion for the unborn. Vice President Mike

---

35 Michael Collins, "GOP challenger Zelenik says Diane Black voted to fund health-care reform," PolitiFact Tennessee, July 27, 2012, http://www.politifact.com/tennessee/statements/2012/jul/27/lou-ann-zelenik/gop-challenger-zelenik-says-diane-black-voted-fund.

36 Chris Bundgaard, "Super PAC in Black-Zelenik races draw national attention," WKRN.com, July 25, 2012, http://wkrn.com/2012/07/25/super-pac-in-black-zelenik-races-draw-national-attention.

Pence handed off his pro-life legislation to her to advance in Congress when he left to run for governor of Indiana because she had been so effective. A tireless supporter for the cause of life, Diane is an active member of the House Pro-life Caucus and the House Values Action Team, and she served as the vice chair of the House GOP's Doctor's Caucus.

In 2013, she sponsored H.R. 940, the Health Care Conscience Rights Act, which seeks to protect medical service providers who have a moral or religious objection to participating in abortions and exempts employers from covering abortions or abortion-inducing drugs in their health insurance plans. Fifty of her House GOP colleagues cosponsored the bill.

"The [Obama] administration has leveraged its expansion of government to trample on the religious freedom of private individuals, hospitals, nonprofits, businesses, churches, and universities—forcing many Americans to make an impossible choice: either defy your religious convictions or break the law and face financially crippling legal penalties," Diane said.[37]

Diane's pro-life position isn't political but a deep personal conviction that stems from her faith and her experience as a nurse. Diane watched a young woman die because she'd had an abortion at a clinic not held to the same health and safety standards as other medical settings. She has since advocated not just for the unborn but also for too many women who

---

37 Joan Frawley Desmond, "Proposed Health Care Conscience Rights Act — 'Last and Only Hope'?", *National Catholic Register*, March 5, 2013.

make the difficult decision to have an abortion and then struggle with the emotional scarring they carry for the rest of their life.

On a frigid day in January of 2013, in recognition of the fortieth anniversary of the *Roe v. Wade* decision, Diane spoke to thousands of pro-life participants at the March for Life demonstration in our nation's capital.

In her speech, Diane said:

On January 22, 1973, the day the Supreme Court handed down the ruling on Roe v. Wade, I was working as a nurse in an emergency room in Baltimore. And this was a time when it was still not widely accepted for women to pursue a career outside the home, or own a business, or maybe even run for elected office. But despite those inroads we have made toward gender equality, abortion on demand continues to undermine the freedom and the justice that generations of women have fought for. The reality is forty years after Roe v. Wade, one-third of my daughters' and granddaughters' peers are not here today to benefit from the progress we've made and to share in our hopes and dreams of the future.

As Martin Luther King Jr. said, "Injustice anywhere is a threat to justice everywhere." For decades pro-abortion activists have perpetrated many lies about abortion, particularly to women.

Lie Number One: We have been told that abortion is merely a means of female liberation, justice, and empowerment. But pitting mothers against the unborn is not liberating. It's a horrible injustice that in the last forty years has resulted in 55 million aborted babies whose mothers have gone on to live in many cases with severe physical, emotional, mental, and spiritual scars. Women who have had abortions are 30 percent more likely to face emotional and mental problems. They are 40 percent more likely to have a premature birth and three times more likely to experience drug and alcohol problems during their lifetime. Such lies cannot continue.

Lie Number Two: We have been told that abortion is about choice, but in reality, abortion is a false choice. Abortion leads to the death of a child—robbing society of its future mothers and fathers, nurses and doctors, teachers and scientists—and a choice to take what is not ours to take: the life of another person. It is not a choice at all—it is a mistake.

Lie Number Three: We have been told the lie that a fetus is not a life. But you know what? Medical advances have affirmed what many of us knew in our hearts when that decision was made so many years ago, that the fetus living inside a woman's body is not a blob of tissue—it's a human being! A living, breathing human baby who has a right to life, just like you and me.

Today, forty years after Roe v. Wade, I'm still a registered nurse. My fight for life has shifted from the emergency room to the Tennessee State Capitol to the halls of Congress. And I'm committed to using whatever opportunities of power and influence that my current position affords me to protect and defend the sanctity of life. And [one of my current efforts has been] to defund the largest abortion provider in America—also known as Planned Parenthood. According to the most recent report Planned Parenthood put out, they've provided three hundred thousand abortions just in this last year. That's one abortion every ninety-four seconds. And you know what—taxpayers' money has unwittingly helped foot the bill for this. Planned Parenthood receives more than a half billion taxpayer dollars annually for what's intended to be women's health money, but it badly misuses this money to subsidize a big abortion business.

And that is why, at the start of this new year with the blessing of my good friend and your good friend Congressman Mike Pence, who is now the governor of Indiana, who has fought for so many years, has handed me over H.R. 217, the Title X Abortion Provider Prohibition Act. If signed into law, my bill would ensure that the Title X federal grants are used for their intended purpose of strengthening families and providing critical health services for women and would bar those dollars from going to organizations that provide abortions.

On this fortieth anniversary of Roe v. Wade, we remember those tens of millions of babies who will never be able to celebrate a birthday, who will not go to college, who won't contribute their God-given talents to this world, and our thoughts and prayers are with those countless men and women whose lives have been forever changed by the violence of abortion. Today we press on for the fight for life and the hope that one day we will live in a country where each and every life, born and unborn, is respected, valued, and given the opportunity to pursue their dreams.

It's no secret that Diane has long been opposed to Planned Parenthood. Prior to her election to Congress, she sponsored legislation in the Tennessee General Assembly, Senate Bill 2686, which prohibited taxpayer-funded coverage for abortion affiliated with impending changes to federal health-care law, which overwhelmingly passed both state houses. It mattered to her that tax dollars not be allotted to any elective abortions in our state. The year before Senate Bill 2686 passed, Diane had also sponsored a successful state budget measure to defund Planned Parenthood by ensuring that any funds designated for family planning were distributed to women's health service providers first.

Two years after Diane made that moving speech at the March for Life, people across the nation were shocked at the revelation of undercover videos that showed doctors and administrators for Planned Parenthood discussing the sale of fetal tissue and body parts. In response, Diane authored the Defund Planned Parenthood Act of 2015, which would block all federal funding from going to any organizations that perform abortions, especially the nation's largest abortion provider. Though her end goal has always been to defund Planned Parenthood entirely, this particular bill was slated to suspend funding for one year while Congress investigated the allegations that Planned Parenthood was not only illegally profiting from the sale of fetal tissue but was also conducting illegal partial-birth abortions. Diane's legislation intended to increase public health funding during that one-year period and redirect funds to the twelve hundred health centers around the country who provide women's health services but do not perform abortions, like faith-based clinics and local health departments.

"I want to see this money actually go to local community health centers so that women can get the medical care they need," Diane said.[38]

She was also a cosponsor of the 2017 Pain-Capable Unborn Child Protection Act, which criminalizes abortions after twenty weeks except in cases of rape or incest or when abortion is necessary to save the life of the mother.

A path to prosperity

After her initial arrival in Congress, Diane's fellow first-year colleagues elected her to serve as the freshman class representative to the Republican Policy Committee, a forum where Republicans discuss and advance legislative initiatives. She was also one of only two freshmen selected to serve on the powerful House Ways and Means Committee, which was very unusual but was in recognition of her success at the state level. House Ways and Means Committee members work on health-care laws, as well as the nation's tax, trade, and welfare legislation. She was also selected to serve on the House Budget Committee as an appointee from Ways and Means.

True to her core principles, Diane has spent her time in Washington focused on fiscal restraint and market-based, patient-centered health-care policy. She demonstrated her unstoppable spirit by becoming the only newly elected Republican congressman of the 2010 group to pass a bill that

---

38 Tena Lee, "Black announces bid for governor," *Hendersonville Standard*, August 2, 2017.

President Obama signed into law. The legislation, H.R. 2576, closed a wasteful loophole in the Affordable Care Act that allowed people with higher incomes to receive a Medicaid subsidy.

"Medicaid is already one of those programs that is having a hard time being funded both at the federal and the state level. It is a program that is meant for people who are at the very lowest level, in poverty, as a safety net for them," Diane told a reporter for *The Hill.* "If you're giving those benefits to somebody at a much higher income, that does not make sense. [H.R. 2576] saved the American taxpayer $13 billion."[39]

She later cosponsored H.R. 277, the American Health Care Reform Act of 2017, which would repeal the ACA altogether and offer a comprehensive conservative alternative.

Diane is a firm believer that getting America's fiscal house in order requires reforming the broken congressional budget process, and she's a strong supporter of zero-based budgeting. That is why she cosponsored a balanced budget amendment to the Constitution, which would prohibit government spending beyond revenues. For added incentive, she was also a co-sponsor of the No Budget, No Pay Act, which withholds pay from Congress if an annual budget is not passed by the law's deadline.

As a member of the House Budget Committee, she helped craft the House Republican's proposed federal budget. During

---

39 Sterling C. Beard, "Rep. Black's healthcare prescription doesn't include the government," *The Hill,* July 30, 2012.

the time Diane has served on the House Budget Committee, the House has passed a budget every year, and in 2017, the House Budget Committee passed two budgets to the floor.

After Tom Price was confirmed as Secretary of Health and Human Services, Diane rose to chairman of the House Budget Committee, becoming the first woman to hold the position. In January of 2017, under her leadership as budget chair, the House passed a budget, which led to the repeal and replace of the Affordable Care Act through reconciliation.

Later in the year, Diane led the way on the most complicated and important budget in decades, which was also the most conservative budget in twenty years. It increased defense spending by $70 billion, balanced the federal budget in ten years, and paved the way for once-in-a-generation tax reform. The fiscal-year 2018 budget resolution also set spending levels for defense and non-defense, allowing Congress to go about the traditional appropriations process for the first time in a decade. The most notable piece of Diane's budget resolution was the reconciliation for tax reform, which represents the first time in thirty years that Congress has attempted to completely rewrite the tax code. Her budget also has reconciliation instructions to eleven authorizing committees to find at least $203 billion in mandatory spending cuts. The last time Congress pursued this level of mandatory spending cuts was the balanced budget deal of 1997.[40]

---

40 Contributed by Chris Hartline, former House Budget Committee aide, November 2017.

Diane's conservative mettle has not gone unnoticed: In 2014, the *National Journal* named her one of the fifteen most conservative congressmen, and in 2015 *CQ Roll Call* named her one of the twenty-five most influential women in Congress. In 2016, she earned the Award for Conservative Excellence from the American Conservative Union, known best as the host of the annual Conservative Political Action Conference (CPAC). (For a comprehensive list of Diane's honors and awards, see the Appendix.)

"The awards ceremonies and scorecards in Washington, DC, are many, but this honor from the American Conservative Union is deeply meaningful to me because it confirms that I have done exactly what I said I would," Diane said in a statement. "Whether it has been my votes to defund Planned Parenthood, halt our refugee resettlement program, or oppose [2015's] bloated omnibus bill, Tennesseans know that I match my conservative rhetoric with a conservative record."

At every turn, Diane has considered how to best serve the constituents who entrusted her with their values, goals, and hopes for the future. She soon came to realize that her heart for this special vocation was now leading her back to state government.

CHAPTER 8

FAITH IN OUR TENNESSEE FUTURE

After four terms in the US House of Representatives, Diane found herself ready to return to Tennessee to invest more directly in the health and prosperity of our home state.

Diane and I both love Tennessee—we've been here more than thirty years now, and this state is home and always will be. Tennessee is truly a special place. We love the warmth of the people, the strong family values, the prevalence of the Christian faith, the friendliness of strangers who wave even if they don't know you. We certainly appreciate that Tennessee is business-friendly and doesn't burden its residents with excessive taxes.

The same year that Diane first took up her seat in the US House of Representatives, Bill Haslam took up residence in the Tennessee governor's mansion. Now that Gov. Haslam's second term is coming to a close, it's time for Tennessee to elect its next governor. Diane is proud to have been a member of the General Assembly for twelve years, and her pursuit of the Tennessee governor's office is the next step in a natural unfolding of her love for this state and her desire to serve its people in unique and effective ways.

Quite some time before Diane decided to enter the gubernatorial race, she got an intriguing word of encouragement from her dear friend Cathy.

"You need to run for governor," Cathy said in a text message.

"Where in the world did that come from?" Diane asked.

"Well, God woke me up in the middle of the night last night and told me to tell you this."

"You're nuts."

"No, I'm not nuts."

"Did God tell you how hard it would be?"

"Yes," replied Cathy, "it's going to be very hard. But you're going to do it."

When their mutual friend Barb found out about this conversation, she told Diane, "You need to pay attention to Cathy because God really does wake her up in the middle of the night and tell her stuff."

Cathy assured Diane that she hadn't been thinking about the governor's race at all, but that's just what came out—she truly sensed God speaking to her in the depths of night to encourage Diane to do the seemingly impossible.

"I'm glad God's talking to you because He sure hasn't talked to me yet," said Diane.

"Maybe you need to listen a bit better," suggested Cathy.

After this divine nudge, Diane and I prayed about whether she should run for governor. I have to admit I wasn't onboard initially because I would rather have her home with me and be available to travel and spend more time with our grandchildren. Eventually, however, we sensed in our spirits that this was truly the right thing to do, and I will always support Diane in her calling to serve our community, our state, and our nation.

In her campaign video, Diane says: "Most people in politics say the right things, but never fight for the right things. They're too meek, or maybe too weak. We believe in absolute truths. Right is right. Wrong is wrong. Truth is truth. God is God. A life is a life. And we don't back down from any of it. That's exactly the kind of governor I will be."

The number one job for our next governor will simply be to fight for what's right and to be unstoppable in defense of all that is right about Tennessee.

A vision for the future

We have faith in the future of Tennessee—our state has experienced tremendous growth and improvements over the past decade. Much of Tennessee's progress and prosperity in recent years, however, has centered in and around Middle Tennessee. We have a serious task before us in extending economic growth to the rural counties, which are plagued by job scarcity, depressed development, and a drug abuse problem that includes the opioid crisis.

These counties need investment in infrastructure, transportation, and job creation. Historically, the commissioner of economic and community development has always brought in large corporations, but this strategy ignores the fact that 70 to 80 percent of jobs are created by small businesses. We shouldn't ignore the big companies, but we should focus on policies that ease regulations and improve tax structures that impact small businesses. We need to also focus our efforts on companies that have been founded in Tennessee by Tennesseans. Government policies should not be only about attracting new businesses from out of state, but supporting our homegrown entrepreneurs who have risked their savings to build their dream businesses.

As governor, Diane plans to focus on bringing jobs, low taxes and prosperity to every corner of Tennessee. She'll be getting help from one of the country's foremost economic experts, Dr. Arthur Laffer, the architect of President Ronald Reagan's fiscal policy.

"Diane Black knows exactly how to keep Tennessee's economy growing rapidly by ensuring that Tennessee keeps tax rates low while paying its bills and protecting its taxpayers," said Dr. Laffer in a statement. "I moved from California to Tennessee eleven years ago for these very reasons, and I couldn't be happier with my adopted home state. There's no one more qualified and prepared to lead Tennessee into a new era of prosperity than Diane Black."[41]

An essential long-term investment in our economy is our educational system. Diane and I are both big fans of Bill Haslam—as governor, he has done a lot of great things, and one of his greatest achievements has been in moving Tennessee from the bottom of national education rankings more toward the middle of all states. That is a great accomplishment, but Tennessee should be, and can be, in the top ten. Diane is likely to look at school choice, such as charter schools and vouchers for private school to give parents and children options for better educational opportunities and not suffer children trapped in failing school systems. We must think differently and we must think big, or HUGE, as President Trump would say.

If we're going to continue our current economic growth, we have to have the education to prepare people to work in business. A lot of that focus should shift from the four-year degree onto trade and vocational schools. We have to move away from the idea that every child has to have a four-year education and graduate with tens of thousands of dollars in student loan debt. It's important to assess interests and aptitude at an earlier age and steer young people into training programs aligned with their natural abilities while also investing them with the skills sought after by local employers.

---

41 "Conservative economic icon Arthur Laffer endorses Diane Black for Governor," Diane Black for Governor, September 13, 2017, https://www.dianeblack.com/conservative-economic-icon-arthur-laffer-endorses-diane-black-governor.

Throughout her district, Diane has heard from employers that they aren't able to hire staff with proper critical thinking and other essential skill sets that employers need. We have, for example, a shortage of at least seventeen thousand IT professionals in Tennessee—filling these positions is crucial for capitalizing on growing economic opportunities in the technology sector.

While Gov. Haslam was in office, one of the ways legislators sought to improve our state's higher education was by reforming the governance of educational institutions and increasing access to our community colleges.

"Through the Focus on College and University Success Act, we changed the way higher education is governed by allowing the six four-year schools overseen by the Board of Regents to create their own boards. The next governor will tackle the challenge of making sure that approach works," noted Ron Ramsey. "We also put in place the Tennessee Promise so high school graduates can go to a two-year school for free. And it's been proven to be successful."[42]

Diane is a big believer in community colleges—her first degree was an associate's from Anne Arundel Community College in Maryland, near where she grew up. She taught medical terminology for five years at Volunteer State Community College in Gallatin, and she served on the College Foundation Board of Trustees for many years. Community colleges are a great place for young people to begin their

---

42 Interview with Ron Ramsey, October 2017.

education or for older adults to learn new skills—statistics show that many students do much better in that smaller setting where they can evaluate whether college is right for them or whether they'd fare better in a technical or vocational school.

Diane and I demonstrated our commitment to supporting education in Tennessee long before her bid for governor. We're big advocates for education because we have been successful as a consequence of our own educational opportunities. And we know ignorance is the root of all of humanity's problems—disease, bigotry, poor financial policy, and more. We supported a GED program in Gallatin when Charles Robert Bone, Diane's first political opponent, was directing it, and we have given quite a bit to the Volunteer State College Foundation for alternative students—those who pursue degrees later in life.

Our greatest gift, however, was to Vol State for the construction of a new humanities building on the Gallatin campus. Diane and I donated $1 million to the effort, which helped the college secure a matching grant. The sizable gift gave us naming rights to the building, but we weren't about to call it the David and Diane Black Humanities Building. Instead, we chose to add two more names to it, beloved friends of ours who otherwise would never have had the chance to see their name on a university structure.

These two families, the Steinhauers and the Rogans, have been more than just friends—they've become part of our family and we're part of theirs. We met John and Jane Steinhauer at church shortly after moving to Hendersonville, and we met Chet and Clara Rogan after Diane and Clara worked together at the Sumner County Medical Center.

Tommy Rogan was especially close as he and his family provided the food each summer for our company picnic. Although this started small, it eventually grew into feeding hundreds of employees and their families, and everyone looked forward every year to the Rogans' barbecue for our annual event. Very sadly, Tommy passed away after a long illness, but the picnics have continued. The Rogans and the Steinhauers are two families made up of remarkable and caring Christians.

Each of these families took us in and loved us and our children. Despite any superficial differences in our political persuasions or personal backgrounds, we truly care about them and wanted to honor what they've meant to us.

"We've been like a family. It's kind of a love thing that we have with them—a longstanding loveship. We just kind of came together; it was one of those things where love flows out to each other and you pick up on it," said Clara.[43]

We revealed the naming to the Steinhauers and the Rogans at a special dinner hosted by Dr. Jerry Faulker, president of Vol State. We invited both families—who didn't know each other since they were each different parts of our lives—to dinner so we could surprise them with our decision and to make sure they approved. The private room at the Club at Fairvue Plantation in Gallatin was filled with about twenty-five folks getting to know each other and enjoying a meal together.

---

43 Interview with Clara Rogan, October 2017.

"When we came in, they said, 'You sit here, you sit there.' I had no idea what was going on or why I was there—this was a surprise," said Clara. "Dr. Faulkner was talking about different things, then Dave had things he needed to say. I wondered, 'What's going on?' They talked about how they had the opportunity to put the name on the building. When he told us what it was, I was in shock. You can't imagine what it's like. I love it and I appreciate it though."

Though John Steinhauer Jr. died in June of 2016 at the age of ninety, he did get to see his name on the side of the humanities building. John lived a generous and compassionate life and left a rich legacy well before his name appeared on the building—he served four terms as a state representative for Sumner County (the same seat to which Diane was first elected!) and a term as chief bill clerk. He was instrumental in establishing Volunteer State Community College, which opened in 1971. John's daughter, Joni, was Vol State's first student body president. John also fought to build Hendersonville Hospital, where many years later Diane worked in the ER when we first moved to Tennessee.

On September 23, 2016, we attended the ribbon cutting ceremony on the Steinhauer-Rogan-Black Humanities Building, which the students have already come to call the "SRB." The 88,000-square-foot building was a $35 million project and fourteen years in the making. The SRB has twenty-three classrooms, seven computer labs, art studios and a gallery, a recording studio, and many more educational amenities that have enlivened student experience and performance since its opening.[44]

When it comes to charitable giving, Diane and I believe in not letting the right hand know what the left is doing. Both of us being people of faith, we know we are called to do our good works silently and without fanfare. What's important about this story, however, is that Diane has a proven track record of investing her time, energy, and heart into her community's educational organizations, which started long before her time in public office and will continue well into the future.

"Diane is a beautiful, loving, caring person. That means more than anything. She's looking out for everybody, not just her. You can't come between her and the care for other people," added Clara.

A heart for children

Life has always been the top issue for Diane, so it goes without saying that, as governor, she will continue to defend and advance pro-life causes. Being pro-life is about more than just preventing or regulating abortions—it's also about cultivating more opportunities for families to take in and properly care for children. Improving Tennessee's foster care system and greatly streamlining the adoption process are ways she will continue to live out her pro-life values.

---

44 Josh Nelson, "Vol State holds grand opening for new humanities building," *Gallatin News*, September 29, 2016.

In 2004, Diane took a stand when Gov. Bredesen's administration and DCS threatened to stop sending foster children to the Baptist Children's Home (BCH) because the children were required to go to church on Sundays. The government argued for separation of church and state, but Diane argued for the effectiveness and quality of care provided at BCH. She refused to let a cold and uncaring process adversely affect children and their need for a loving and protective environment.

Some of Diane's most memorable involvement in challenging ineffective DCS policies centered on the Sandstrom family. In 2005, Kam and Carol Sandstrom of Christiana, Tennessee, became foster parents of a toddler named Maddie whose young mother felt unable to adequately provide for her.

"We got involved with foster care not necessarily just to foster but for adoption," said Carol. "We hunted down the biological father because he had never been part of Maddie's life, and then we fought for almost a year to adopt her. In the end, the father was able to gain custody of Maddie simply because he was genetically related. Maddie had no clue who this man was, but she was forced to live with him and his wife. They'd just lost an infant son and his wife wanted another baby, which is why he fought to get Maddie."

Within a year, however, Maddie was back with her biological mother again. The Sandstroms were catalyzed into action—their goal was to revise the existing statute on child custody and support so that judges would be allowed to consider nonbiological caregivers when determining custody arrangements in the best interest of the child.

The Sandstroms reached out to State Senator Bill Ketron in Murfreesboro, who referred them to State Representative John Hood, to sponsor what they called Maddie's Law.

"I can sponsor this in the House, but let me talk to some people because you'll need a sponsor in the Senate," replied Rep. Hood.

Rep. Hood got Diane involved, and she jumped right on board. HB 0822 and SB 1147, presented in the 2007-2008 Tennessee legislative session, amended TCA Section 36-6-106 with the simple addition of one word: caregiver. Maddie's Law was passed unanimously.

"At that point, only genetic relationships were being given preference in court, whether the child knew who that person was or not," Carol explained. "That change to the statute opened the door for caregivers to testify at best interest hearings, and it opened the door for judges to rule that a child currently in the custody of someone who was a nonbiological caregiver could maintain that custody if that's where the child's familial ties or sense of bonding was."

The Sandstroms are an amazing family. By the time Maddie's Law was passed, the couple had taken in three boys who were five, six, and eight years old at the time.

"These young guys came from parents who abused drugs and alcohol, severely neglected their medical care, and subjected them to unspeakable traumas," said Carol. "They were in and out of foster care—by the time they moved in with us, the eldest had been in thirteen different foster homes. The boys were almost feral when they moved in, so hyperactive and no real social skills to speak of. At their last foster family, their biggest accomplishment was learning to sit at a table and eat with silverware."

From the beginning, the Sandstroms intended to adopt the children, and the three boys had even chosen new first names as part of the process. But it would be several more years before their adoption became official.

"DCS had at one point put in a no-contact order for the biological mom because she was so disruptive to the kids and she was just not safe. They'd not retracted that, so they couldn't terminate her parental rights based on abandonment, even though she walked off and no one knew where she was for a year," explained Carol.

As a result, DCS had to allow the biological mother to go through a parenting plan to regain custody of the children. While the parenting plan was perhaps a technicality, DCS still gave it a good-faith effort. But the custody hearings and forced interactions with the biological mother devastated the children, resulting in night terrors and regressive behavior. The youngest boy, Wiley, had been in foster care for so long he had no clue who his biological mother was.

Diane was present at numerous foster care review board meetings on behalf of the three boys, beginning when they were in their last foster home in Hendersonville and continuing throughout much of the Sandstroms' adoption battle. Three little boys were falling through the cracks, and she wasn't going to stand for it.

"Here she was in those meetings, this classy lady who inspired everyone to be on their best behavior, yet she was so nonintrusive," noted Carol. "Diane asked key questions about whether particular laws applied to the case, and she initiated conversations other people had advised us not to bring up. She didn't come in guns blazing, but she knew the law, and as a result of her presence, people were careful to follow more strictly the steps that were supposed to be followed."

The boys had been living with the Sandstroms for twenty-nine months when the middle son, Charlie, died in a tragic accident. He was just eight years old.

Charlie and his brothers were fishing at a pond on the Sandstroms' property with his foster father, Kam, and a few family friends when Charlie got overexcited and accidentally poked one of the other boys in the eyelid with his fishing rod. Kam gently advised young Charlie to take a break and settle down a bit. Charlie went to the barn and got bailing twine out of a bucket, which he used in his attempt to build a swing. He slipped off a ledge between the barn and the pond and accidentally hung himself on the rope. Carol's in-laws arrived with snacks and discovered the boy partially visible between the side of the ledge and a retaining wall.

The medical examiner assured the Sandstroms that Charlie hadn't suffered.

"One of the most stabilizing moments of that whole situation was at the visitation when a friend told me, 'Diane Black is here.' When I saw her, she opened up her arms and said, 'My dear sweet friend,' and she hugged me and cried with me," said Carol. "That's what makes her such a strong advocate—she's willing to feel, and there's a huge risk in that for public figures. She truly cares. I love this lady—she will forever be special to our family. I know we're not the only people she's ever helped, but I have no idea how she's had time to help anyone else because she has helped us so much," said Carol.

Diane's commitment to adoption extended into her time in Congress. When the adoption tax credit was first eliminated in the proposed 2018 House budget, she fought to have it reinstated. The tax itself costs the federal government substantially little in comparison to overall revenues, but the credit makes a big impact on families seeking to adopt children in need. Diane also sponsored and introduced the Adoption Tax Credit Refundability Act in May of 2017, which amends the Internal Revenue Code to make the tax credit for adoption expenses refundable. Lower income families who adopt may not qualify for the adoption tax credit because they don't have the tax liability; many of them are 200 percent below the poverty line. But her bill allows the amount of the credit to be refundable to help with the unavoidable expenses of adopting a child.

As governor of Tennessee, Diane will take a hard look at DCS's current policies, regulations, and operations. Too many children have fallen through the cracks of the current system, and too many loving, qualified foster families are repeatedly frustrated or hindered from caring for or adopting eligible children.

Christians are called to care for the widows and the orphans, and though not everyone can foster or adopt, there are still ways to support these children. This issue is close to both our hearts—Diane was a single mother struggling to support three young children by working the night shift at a hospital. I loved her children deeply and adopted them as my own. A forever family is what every foster child needs. We need to make adoption easier and less costly for families in Tennessee and across the country.

A servant leader

Diane and I receive a lot of negative comments from people who don't know us because we have been financially successful. But that might just be because these folks don't know where we came from, or how hard we have worked to get to where we are. The truth is we're still basically blue collar. In fact, I like to call myself a "blue-collar redneck." The people we like to hang out with are the people we've always known. We don't try to cultivate relationships because of anyone's economic or social status or location in life. We are still essentially the same people we always were, just a little older.

Another of the accusations lately leveled at Diane is that she's an "establishment politician." The idea that anyone with experience in government is "establishment" is a virulent notion currently plaguing our political discourse. There is certainly a place and a need for disruptors—and Diane has been such a force on numerous occasions—but equally important are people with the skills, knowledge, and relationships to actually accomplish goals. She is both extremely conservative while at the same time pragmatic enough to know how to get things done. She has demonstrated her dedication, intelligence, and aptitude as a legislator at both the state and federal levels.

Most importantly, Diane has a big heart for serving others, and she has demonstrated this over and over again in our community—oftentimes to no public acclaim. The people who know her will testify to this generosity and compassion, particularly those who have worked with her to serve Tennessee's most vulnerable populations.

Fred Bailey, the founder of Children Are People (CAP), is one such fan of Diane's. Fred, who is now sixty-four, was born one of fifteen children to sharecroppers in Gallatin. He was also born with a degenerative eye disease that left him with only minimal light perception by age nine, and he was completely blind by age fifteen. What's exceptional about Fred, however, is that he has never for a moment allowed either his poverty or his blindness to limit his potential or opportunities in life. He went on to earn a bachelor's degree from Tennessee State University and worked for General Electric.[45] Fred coached wrestling for middle school and high school students before starting his nonprofit, which

---

45 For more about Fred Bailey and Children Are People, visit www. childrenarepeopletn.org.

exists to mentor and empower at-risk children in Sumner County.

"I wanted to work with young people and show them what it would take to function well in America and especially in a democratic capitalistic system. Color and gender won't make a difference in how you function—a good name and a good character is what matters. That's how it started," said Fred.[46]

Fred first met Diane back in 2000 at a Young Republicans meeting in Sumner County, and the two immediately hit it off.

"Diane served on our board of directors for six to eight years until she got too busy and was traveling, but even before she got on the board she was helping me," said Fred. "I really didn't have a place to start this organization— no building or anything. I remember she'd come and pick me up in a little two-seater car. She used to move a mile a minute. When she walked, you better be in good shape just to keep up with her! We'd ride all around Gallatin trying to find a suitable building to start CAP. I worked her to death. You'd think she was my chauffeur; she drove me all over the place."

Diane loved what Children Are People stood for and the positive difference it was making in the lives of children in her district. In 2015, she arranged for a group of thirty-five of Fred's middle school and high school students to take a trip to Washington, DC.

---

46 Interview with Fred Bailey, October 2017.

"These kids have grown up on the streets and in public housing—this was the first time some of them had ever been out of Gallatin, let alone out of the state," explained Fred. "For a kid who doesn't know how to dream, the seat of power means nothing. But then they visited DC, Arlington, the Smithsonian—they saw monuments they'd only read about in books. Now as a child, each of them could put it all in perspective, there in the midst of it. It made social studies come to life. To go there was monumental for these kids' growth. And Diane made all that happen."

The kids returned to Gallatin with a newfound perspective of the United States and of what it means to be in America. They understood that even though their circumstances may be meager, noted Fred, with a little initiative and a strong character, they could get somewhere in this country.

Fred pointed out how essential Diane's efforts were to the success of the DC field trip.

"She's a big financial benefactor for us, and she was the primary funder for this trip. She always does things for us. If I had ten partners like Diane, Children Are People would be in every city in this country. She's wanted to take it nationally for a long time. She loves what we do. As busy as she is, to take that time, to do what this organization asks of her, is dedication," he said.

Another local leader who has been blessed by Diane's friendship and involvement is Lori Kissinger, a musician, educator, and executive director of what's now called

Borderless Arts Tennessee, a nonprofit organization that produces art and music programs to benefit and empower people with disabilities.[47] Lori first met Diane in the spring of 2004 when Lori's third-grade son, Christian, was part of Little Volunteers, an organization run by the Junior Service League of Gallatin. After learning about the history of Sumner County and Tennessee, the children put together a self-published book about their educational experience and presented it to Diane, their state representative at the time.

"Diane liked the book so much she asked the officers of Little Volunteers—and Christian was president—to come present it on the floor at the Tennessee legislature," said Lori. "She and Christian ended up really hitting it off, and she told him about being a page for a day. Usually pages were high school students, but if he wanted to try it he could, and he said yes."

Lori said that her most vivid memory of Diane happened the day she and Christian arrived for the page-for-a-day program.

"We were sitting in her outer office while Diane was in her office on a phone call. The person on the other line was just screaming at her—so loudly that we could hear this person in the lobby area and even part of what they were saying," said Lori. "Diane remained very calm throughout the whole conversation; she never got nasty or angry or raised her voice. She made the comment to them that she had certain views and ethical values, and as long as the people of

---

47 For more about Borderless Arts Tennessee, visit borderlessartstn.org.

Tennessee voted for her to hold those values, that's what she was going to do. And when those values were no longer the values of her constituents, then they wouldn't vote her in. I found that to be insightful of her to not argue the point. She just reiterated her views and values. I appreciated that."

Once Diane got to know Lori and the mission of her arts organization, she joined the board of directors for several years and singlehandedly funded one of the nonprofit's signature initiatives, the young soloist program. In 2006, Diane helped Borderless Arts Tennessee partner with the Department of Education, which extended the group's impact across Tennessee.

"We were featuring young people with disabilities on the stage at the Ryman, and we had bussed in special education classes from all over Metro Nashville," Lori explained. "Diane was impressed with this program and connected us with the commissioner of the Department of Education. They came to a performance and were so impressed that it led to a partnership with the Department of Education that still stands today. We get contracts from them to do residencies in special education classes across the state because of the connection Diane made for us."

In another instance, Diane arranged for a group of young people with disabilities from Westmoreland to come speak at the statehouse—kids who had never been out of Sumner County in their lives. She rented a motor coach to bring the kids to Nashville and, after their time visiting the state

Senate, took them to dinner at the Spaghetti Factory. Some of the kids had never eaten in a restaurant that wasn't fast food before.

One young boy said, "This is the most beautiful place I've ever been. If I ever get married, I'm going to propose to my wife right here."

Lori and Diane have known each other for many years now, and Lori gets riled up by the accusations she hears hurled at her friend.

"Diane doesn't need the money or the glory or the fame. Her rivals or detractors say, 'She's getting this or that benefit.' She doesn't need anything nor is she getting anything out of what she does. She's just trying to help and do things for people. I see her do that in quiet ways no one even knows about or hears about," said Lori. "One of the things that stood out for me in that respect is how she and Dave underwrote that building at Vol State—but their name is listed last. People usually give those donations to have their name first and foremost on the building. Who pays for a building and puts other people's names on it? Who does that? That's the kind of people the Blacks are."

What Diane does and the gifts she gives are not driven by a quest for power or recognition. On the contrary, as a woman of deep, abiding faith, her goodness is the overflow of a heart rooted and grounded in the love of God.

But you don't have to take my word for it. I'll let our pastor speak on her behalf. Doug Varnado and his wife, Linda, are pastors at Community Church in Hendersonville, where Diane and I have been attend Sunday services since 2009.

"She's just Diane in our church. Not Congressman Diane. Just Diane. A person among us that God is using well. She loves well and loves much and doesn't draw attention to herself. She demonstrates humility—total lack of pride and ego. It's just nonexistent with her," said Doug.

"Diane is so very wise. One day in the hall, we talked about what she was trying to achieve with the House budget. I told her, 'This is way over my head, but I'm thankful you're leading this and kind enough to think I can understand it,' She blows me away with what she grasps," added Linda. "Regardless that she is in politics, she is genuine, which is a rare and beautiful quality. The Blacks are very real. You know who they are and what they stand for even in conversation but also in terms of a shared journey with our church family."

As people of faith, church isn't a sidetrack or an extension but an essential part of our everyday lives. Diane and I have joyfully served our church and the surrounding community in different ways, including Room in the Inn, which is a citywide church collective to offer Christlike hospitality to the homeless, and Operation Christmas Child, which sends shoeboxes full of gifts to needy children around the world.

Diane's faith has been the catalyst for my own spiritual journey, and she inspires others in our church as well.

"Diane has the kind of faith that causes her to be very dependent and appreciative of prayer," said Linda. "She really believes God will sustain her through prayer. When you're that talented, you could become independent and believe you had it in yourself, but she's not that way. Her faith is deep and real."

"Diane and I taught together for several years—she's an excellent teacher and student of the Word. She has a high regard for Scripture and a deep faith—a center from which everything radiates," Doug said. "Her faith isn't an affiliated faith but an owned faith. She talks about being with believers in DC, and she gets excited about what they share—seat to the street, heart to the hands—a practical application. Having been a nurse, she is strong as iron but compassionate and sensitive too. She's a tremendous listener, which not many people are."[48]

Diane indeed is strong as iron but loving and compassionate. As Fred Bailey noted in our interview, if you only ever take in the media perspective, you'll never understand who she is. She is where she is because of her work ethic and inner drive and her deep desire to make a difference in people's lives.

"The thing about Diane that makes her so different is that she is so real. Her heart is so huge and wide open and she loves so completely. If she cares about you—and she cares about so many people—it is obvious and it is real, and nothing is too much or too little," said Carol.

"Anything Diane has done, she has truly done for the people. She wouldn't be where she is if she didn't think she had something to offer or wasn't going to help her fellow

---

48 Interview with Doug and Linda Varnado, October 2017.

citizens," said Barb. "I think she'll do a fantastic job as governor. Being the first woman, she'll go down in history, but when she finishes her terms, they'll write about what a terrific governor she was."

I have been blessed to be Diane's husband for thirty-seven years and to be the father of her three children, and I am proud to support her in her every effort to serve the people of our great state. Although I am biased and love her deeply, I honestly believe Diane Black is the best candidate to be the next—and first female—governor of Tennessee. She may well be. After all, she is *unstoppable!*

# # #

ABOUT THE AUTHOR

David L. Black, PhD, is an internationally recognized forensic toxicologist, founder of Aegis Sciences Corporation, founder and CEO of the Phoenix Sciences Group LLC, and founder and CEO of 2nd Vote. Dr. Black has served as a consultant to major organizations for development of substance abuse prevention and testing programs. Dr. Black has extensive experience as an expert witness in local, state, national, and international court cases involving drug use and testing.

He earned his undergraduate degree from Loyola College in Baltimore, Maryland, and his doctorate degree in forensic toxicology from the University of Maryland at Baltimore. Dr. Black is a Diplomate of the American Board of Forensic Toxicology (D-ABFT) and a Fellow of the American Institute of Chemists (FAIC). Dr. Black is currently a clinical associate professor with appointments in pathology, microbiology, immunology, and pharmacology at Vanderbilt University.

Prior to attending college, Dr. Black served in the United States Marine Corps and deployed for thirteen months to

South Vietnam from June 1968 to July 1969. He served with 1st Marine Aircraft Wing stationed in Danang and Chu Lai in what was referred to as I Corps, just below the demilitarized zone (DMZ) separating South and North Vietnam. Arriving just as the Tet Offensive of 1968 was concluding, he spent ninety days on night patrol guarding the Danang airbase prior to assignment in the communication command center due to his top secret clearance. Subsequently he was finally assigned to his air wing unit performing avionics maintenance on the A-6 Intruder fighter-bomber. Due to a noncombat injury sustained in September of 1968, Dr. Black is a 10 percent disabled veteran.

Dr. Black and his wife, Diane, have been married for more than thirty-seven years. They have three grown children and six grandchildren. They live in Gallatin and attend Community Church in Hendersonville.

Note from the Author

Profits from the sale of this book will be donated to the following nonprofit programs. Readers are encouraged to donate and support these organizations that are making a great difference in healing a fallen and wounded world.

Borderless Arts Tennessee is an arts program for people with disabilities to enrich creative expression, empower career development, and encourage community engagement.
https://borderlessartstn.org/

Children Are People is an after-school mentoring program for at-risk children.
https://www.care.com/b/l/children-are-people-inc/gallatin-tn

Decisions, Choices & Options provides classroom training and prevention education for students on topics of teen pregnancy and abstinence.
https://dcoinc.org/

The Jason Foundation is dedicated to the prevention of youth suicide through educational and awareness programs. http://jasonfoundation.com/

REBOOT Combat Recovery is a faith-based combat-trauma healing course designed to address PTSD and the spiritual wounds of war.
https://rebootrecovery.com/

ACKNOWLEDGEMENTS

This book would not have been written without the input and assistance from many special people. I have had great help to keep the information as accurate as possible and to protect against the normal lapses of memory that occur with the passing of time. Any errors of commission or omission are my responsibility alone and have occurred despite a best effort to provide an honest narrative.

I cannot name everyone who has assisted with this project, but several must be mentioned. This book would have not come to life without the guidance and advice of David Dunham, the fact checking of Lance Frizzell, the legal guidance of John Gall, the review and critique of our dear friends Aaron and Charlotte Elkins, and the generous contributions of dear friends who provided stories and memories. I am grateful to all and acknowledge that this book could not have been completed without our extended family who love Diane almost as much as I do!

APPENDIX

COMMUNITY SERVICE

Teacher, Adult Sunday School

Alumni Member, Leadership Middle Tennessee

Past president, Hendersonville Morning Rotary Club Foundation

Board Member, Children Are People Inc.

Board Member, Volunteer State Community College Foundation

Board Member, Borderless Arts Tennessee

Past Chair, United Way of Sumner County

Past Board Member, YMCA

Past Board Member, Hendersonville Chamber of Commerce

Past Board Member, American Heart Association for Sumner County

Past President, Leadership Sumner Alumni Association

Past Vice Chair, Habitat for Humanity of Sumner County

Past President, Nashville Area Women of the ELCA

Past President, P.E.O. International

Past President, Hendersonville Rotary Club

Past President, Gallatin Chapter, American Cancer Society

Past President, Gallatin Toastmasters

Member, National Rifle Association

Member, Leadership Sumner Association

Past Member, Gallatin, Goodlettsville, Hendersonville, Portland, Springfield/Robertson, Westmoreland, and White House Chambers of Commerce

Past Member, League of Women Voters

Past Member, Youth Alive & Free Advisory Board

LEGISLATIVE SERVICE

Chair, State Senate Republican Caucus

Member, State Senate Judiciary Committee

Member, State Senate General Welfare, Health and Human Resources Committee

Member, State Senate Finance, Ways and Means Committee

Member, State Senate Select Committee on Children and Youth

Member, State Senate Long-Term Care Oversight Committee

Member, Steering Committee for the Republican Study Committee (RSC)

Member, Congressional Tea Party Caucus

Member, Congressional Pro-Life Caucus

Member, US House Ways & Means Committee

Chair, US House Budget Committee

HONORS AND AWARDS

Girl of the Year, Local Optimist Club, 1969

Who's Who in Community Colleges, 1990

Faculty Award, Belmont University, 1992

Service Above Self Award, 1992

Rotarian of the Year, Hendersonville Rotary Club, 1993

Joy Lomax Martin Award, 1997

Leadership Sumner Distinguished Alumni, 1998

Sumner County YMCA Volunteer of the Year, 2001

American Cancer Society Legislator of the Year, 2003

Right to Life Legislator of the Year, 2004

Recognized by Sumner County Chapter 240 Vietnam Veterans, 2005

County Officials Association of Tennessee Outstanding
State Senator, 2005

Tennessee Nurses Association Outstanding Legislator of
the Year, 2005

American Heart Association Advocate of the Year, 2006

American Diabetes Association State Public Policy
Leadership Award, 2007

Sumner County Ladies Delegation First Woman Senate
Republican Caucus Chairman, 2007

Henry Toll Fellowship Program Class of 2007

Emerging Leader Class of 2007

Recognized by Tennessee Suicide Prevention Network, 2007

Junior Leagues of Tennessee Legislator of the Year, 2008

Tennessee Home Education Association Statesman Award,
2008

Farmers Insurance Group, Outstanding Legislative &
Community Service, 2008

The Arc of Tennessee Legislature Award, 2008

Tennessee Development District Association Legislator of
the Year Award, 2008

Recognized by the Tennessee Organ Donor Registry, 2008

Assisted Living Federation of American Champions for
Seniors in Assisted Living Award, 2008

Tennessee Association of Homes & Services for the Aging Honorary Chair Award, 2008

National Federation of Independent Business Guardian of Small Business Award, 2008

American Heart Association Legislator of the Year, 2008

Tennessee Association of Assessing Officers Legislator of the Year, 2008

National Right to Life, 100% Pro-Life Rating

Tennessee Association of Homes & Services for the Aging, Champion for Seniors in Assisted Living Award

National Federation of Independent Business, Guardian Award, 2011

Association of Building Contractors Champion of Merit Shop, 2011

Friend of the Farm Bureau of Tennessee Award, 2011

Competitive Enterprise Institute 100 percent Pro-worker Voting Score, Fall 2011 Congressional Labor Scorecard

Platinum Prescription by the House Republican Conference, 2012

Association of Building Contractors Champion of Merit Shop, 2013

Friend of the Farm Bureau of Tennessee Award, 2013

NAM Award for Manufacturing Legislative Excellence, 2013

Child Health Advocacy Institute, Champion for Children's Health, 2013

National Association of Community Health Centers, Distinguished Community Health Advocate Award, 2013

FreedomWorks Award for Action to Achieve Conservative Wins in Congress, 2013

International Foodservice Distributors Association, Thomas Jefferson Award, 2014

Visiting Nurse Associations of America Congressional Champion, 2014

Award for Conservative Achievement by the ACU, 2014

Healthcare Leadership Council, Champion of Healthcare Innovation Award, 2014

National Federation of Independent Business, Guardian Award, 2015

Tennessee Chapter of Children's Advocacy Centers, Child Protection Investigative Team Leadership Award

Twenty-five Most Influential Women in Congress, CQ Roll Call, 2015

Friend of the Farm Bureau of Tennessee Award, 2015

Affordability Champion for Efforts to Reduce the Cost of Healthcare for All Americans, 2015

Toy Industry Association Champion of Play, 2015

National Taxpayers Union, Taxpayers' Friend Award, 2015

American College of Rheumatology, Award for Public Leadership in Rheumatology, 2015

Family Research Council Action, True Blue Award, 2015

Healthcare Leadership Council, Champion of Healthcare Innovation Award, 2015

Award for Conservative Excellence, American Conservative Union, 2016

FreedomWorks Award for Action to Achieve Conservative Wins in Congress, 2016

International Foodservice Distributors Association, Thomas Jefferson Award, 2016

Spirit of Enterprise Award, 2016

National Retail Federation Award for Continued Support of the Retail Industry, 2016

Home Instead Senior Care, Senior Advocate Changing the Face of Aging, 2016

VSA Tennessee (now Borderless Arts Tennessee), Young Soloist Supporter Award, 2016

Boy Scouts of America, Good Scout Award, 2016

Healthcare Leadership Council, Champion of Healthcare Innovation Award, 2016

Campaign to End Obesity Champion, 2017

American Bakers Association, Bakers' Dozen Award, 2017

Susan B. Anthony List: Marilyn Musgrave Defender of Life Award, 2017

FreedomWorks Award for Action to Achieve Conservative Wins in Congress, 2017

FRC Action, True Blue Award, 2017

YMCA Congressional Champion Award, 2017

US Chamber of Commerce, Spirit of Enterprise Award, 2017

ACU's Award for Conservative Excellence, 2017